Does Your Program Measure Up?

Does Your Program Measure Up?

An Addiction Professional's Guide for Evaluating Treatment Effectiveness

JERRY SPICER

HAZELDEN®

First published February 1991.

ISBN: 0-89486-698-2
Library of Congress Catalog Card Number: 90-84091

Printed in the United States of America.

Editor's note:
Hazelden Educational Materials offers a variety of information on chemical dependency and related areas. Our publications do not necessarily represent Hazelden programs, nor do they officially speak for any Twelve Step organization.

About the author:

Jerry Spicer, Chief Operating Officer of the Hazelden Foundation, directs the operations of Hazelden's rehabilitation, publishing, and professional services, as well as serving as President of Hazelden Services, Inc. and Hanley/Hazelden Center at St. Mary's and as a member of Hazelden's Board of Directors. He is also a member of the American College of Healthcare Executives and the American College of Addiction Treatment Administrators. He holds masters degrees in sociology and in hospital administration. His special interests are in research, health care administration, training, and writing. He has been the author of twenty articles and four books, including *The EAP Solution* and *Counseling Ethnic Minorities,* both published by Hazelden Educational Materials.

CONTENTS

Acknowledgments   xiii

Preface   xv

PART I

SETTING THE STAGE

Chapter One:

TREATMENT MODELS
AND OUTCOME EVALUATION   3

J. Clark Laundergan, Ph.D.

In this chapter, Dr. Laundergan sets the stage for later discussions by reviewing the more common models and theories used in describing and treating chemical dependency. Although research methods are presumed to assure objectivity, what we study and the questions we ask are influenced by our beliefs about alcoholism and other drug abuse. Although the Minnesota Model may be the most widely used model, it is less studied than other approaches that lend themselves to more experimental and measurable research designs.

Chapter Two:

CHEMICAL DEPENDENCY RESEARCH   19

Patricia Owen, Ph.D.

Dr. Owen writes of the complexities of chemical dependency to be taken into account when trying to determine treatment success. These include the difficulty of diagnosing the disease, the variables in treatment, the substance of the research sample, the denial factor, and the problem of geographic moves. She also raises the question of categorizing a slip and reminds us of the personality factors and the individual's life after treatment that constitute true recovery.

PART II

EVALUATING TREATMENT FROM ADMISSION TO AFTERCARE

Chapter Three:

WHAT IS EVALUATION?   29

Jerry Spicer

A definition of evaluation begins this chapter, and the author cites reasons for evaluating. He gives illustrations of types of evaluation approaches and the goals they may accomplish; explores the differences between evaluation and research; looks at the impact evaluation can have on planning and managing a treatment program; and concludes by examining the limitations and advantages of follow-up surveys.

Chapter Four:

THE PLANNING STAGES   39

Jerry Spicer

The author describes decisions that precede the creation of a follow-up evaluation system. These include assembling a planning committee of people affected by the study, listing the objective, setting goals, and developing a budget.

Chapter Five:

THE FOLLOW-UP SYSTEM   45

Jerry Spicer

After the planning stages, the typical treatment program is ready to begin preparing for an evaluation. The author gives an overall view of the decisions that must be made to conduct a study, including the methods of survey, setting the sample size, and designing a questionnaire. He concludes with sections on data analysis and the importance of pre-testing.

Chapter Six:

ADDRESSING SPECIAL ISSUES   63

Jerry Spicer

Once everything is set in motion toward conducting a survey, special issues and problems may put impediments in the path. Contracts with consultants must be negotiated, reliability checks must be set in place, ethical issues may crop up, and staff may be dragging their feet. This chapter contains sage advice for anticipating and countering such obstacles.

PART III

FUTURE TRENDS

Chapter Seven:

LINKING QUALITY ASSURANCE AND OUTCOME EVALUATION   75

Jerry Spicer

Though, historically, in treatment programs, quality assurance and patient outcome have been divided functions, they appear to be merging in accountability. The author reports on this trend as it takes into consideration factors such as client satisfaction and extending treatment responsibility to aftercare programs.

Chapter Eight:

INFORMATION MANAGEMENT IN THE CHEMICAL DEPENDENCY TREATMENT FIELD 77

Donald Jones and Kevin Johnson

In easy-to-understand language, the authors explain a management information system (MIS) and its application to a chemical dependency treatment program. Many of us may be unaware that an MIS does not necessarily require a computer, but if that is your aim, practical steps to prepare staff for computerization are listed. The authors also offer detailed tips for choosing both hardware and software, as well as choosing consultants. This is, in all, a comprehensive account.

PART IV

CASE STUDIES

Chapter Nine:

TREATMENT OUTCOMES FOR
MINNESOTA MODEL PROGRAMS   93

Paul Higgins, Ph. D.; Ruth Baeumler;
Jeanne Fisher; and Victoria Johnson

With a wealth of tables and figures, this chapter demonstrates the valuable data that can be gathered from surveys evaluating treatment, quality of post-treatment life, and other information that also lends itself to quality assurance. The data are compiled from the Hazelden Evaluation Consortium, consisting of fourteen members, and includes information from seven of those programs, in addition to Hazelden. The data illustrates how program evaluation lends itself to new insights.

Chapter Ten:

THE CHEMICAL ABUSE TREATMENT
OUTCOME REGISTRY (CATOR): TREATMENT
OUTCOME FOR PRIVATE PROGRAMS   115

Norman G. Hoffmann, Ph.D., and
Patricia Ann Harrison, M.A.

One of the nation's largest outcome evaluation systems, CATOR is a service of the Ramsey Clinic Department of Psychiatry in St. Paul, Minnesota. This chapter discusses follow-up information gleaned from samples of two groups of patients CATOR studied. The authors point out significant correlations in many areas and they also do a comprehensive exploration of selection bias.

Chapter Eleven:

ADOLESCENT CHEMICAL DEPENDENCY
TREATMENT OUTCOME RESEARCH   135

Patricia Owen, Ph.D., and Ken C. Winters, Ph. D.

In this case study, the authors review existing adolescent chemical dependency treatment outcome research and discuss future research needs. Their first—"Existing Research"—section presents an overview of existing outcome studies of adolescent populations. Their second section—"Research Issues"—discusses general considerations when conducting outcome research, with an emphasis on the differences between adults and adolescents.

Chapter Twelve:

COST ANALYSES OF
CHEMICAL DEPENDENCY TREATMENT   155

Norman G. Hoffmann, Ph.D., and Jerry Spicer

Recently, research in chemical dependency treatment has shifted its focus to include financial impact. The authors review the concepts, methods, and findings of cost analysis. With definitions of terms, and graphics demonstrating the long-term savings gained in many areas by treating people for chemical dependency, the authors give valuable insights for treatment administrators.

Chapter Thirteen:

COMPARISON OF HAZELDEN
INPATIENT AND OUTPATIENT PROGRAMS   181

Thomas McKenna, Ph.D.;
Leslie Tamble; and Jerry Spicer

This study is a reprint of *Apples and Oranges: A Comparison of Inpatient and Outpatient Treatment Programs,* published by Hazelden in 1981. Although it is an older study, the results are consistent with current issues and are appropriate to today's debates about the differences between residential and outpatient programs. A significant advantage of this study is that the two programs studied were based on the same program philosophy and model of care—the only differences were the setting and patient characteristics. Outpatient care is often cited as the cost effective option to residential care, but as Chapter Twelve illustrated, the cost benefit question is more complex that assumed by critics of residential treatment.

Epilogue   187

Appendix A: Consultation Services   189

Appendix B: Sample Instruments   193

Bibliography   207

Index   213

ILLUSTRATIONS

FIGURES

3.1 Examples of evaluation options 32
3.2 Evaluation/research continuum 33

4.1 Budgeting for a one-year follow-up survey 42
4.2 Sample budget—third year.....................................43

5.1 Documentation 46
5.2 Wording of questions..51
5.3 Follow-up areas 52
5.4 Sample follow-up survey coding system...................54
5.5 Patients not improved...60

9.1 The consortium's average alcohol and
    other drug abstinence rates at six vs. twelve
    months post-treatment 108
9.2 The consortium's average AA/NA attendance
    at six vs. twelve months post-treatment...............109

12.1 Cost-analyses terms 157
12.2 Cost-effectiveness example 161
12.3 Average monthly total medical care costs per
     family—1973–1979: Blue Cross-Blue Shield of
     California enrollees from state employees 169
12.4 Use of health care services before and after
     chemical dependency treatment...........................170
12.5 Days of hospitalization before and after
     chemical dependency treatment 173
12.6 Alcohol- and other drug-related occupational
     problems before and after chemical
     dependency treatment..175
12.7 Other problems before and after chemical
     dependency treatment..176

TABLES

5.1 Present AA Attendance Twelve Months After
Treatment 56

5.2 Helpfulness of Services One Year After
Treatment 57

5.3 Comparison of Sustained Abstinence Rates
For Regular and Non-regular Discharges................58

5.4 Patient and Significant Other Responses
To Similar Questions at Eight Months After
Treatment 59

9.1 Patient Profile 100

9.2 Chemical Dependency Problem at Time Of
Admission..101

9.3 Treatment Profile 103

9.4 Follow-Up Survey Response Rates........................104

9.5 Alcohol and Illicit Drug Use at Six Months
Post-Treatment..105

9.6 Alcohol and Illicit Drug Use at Twelve Months
Post-Treatment..106

9.7 Attendance at AA/NA Meetings At
Six vs. Twelve Months Post-Treatment..................110

9.8 Change in Overall Quality of Life From
Pre-Treatment to Six Months Post-Treatment 111

9.9 Change in General Enjoyment of Life from
Pre-Treatment to Twelve Months Post-Treatment..111

10.1 Sociodemographics of Two CATOR Groups............118

10.2 Substance Use Frequency During the Year
Preceding Treatment..120

10.3 Abstinence After Treatment 122

11.1 Drug Abuse Reporting Program (DARP)................137

11.2 Treatment Outcome Prospective Study (TOPS).....139

11.3 Pennsylvania Substance Abuse System:
Uniform Data Collection System (UDCS)................141

11.4 Chemical Abuse Treatment Outcome Registry
(CATOR)..143

12.1 Hospital Days Utilized..172

12.2 Vocational Functioning Before and After
Chemical Dependency Treatment 176

ACKNOWLEDGMENTS

Many people have supported the writing of this book. Colleagues, staff, and clients from many different programs and projects have provided their insights, and others have contributed valuable time by writing portions of, and reviewing, the book. I would also like to express my appreciation to the American College of Addiction Treatment Administrators for supporting this effort as my Fellowship project. Special recognition should be given to Hazelden's administration and board of trustees for their initial and continuing support for research and program evaluation.

PREFACE

A few years ago I attended a workshop on outcome evaluation and follow-up surveys. The workshop was sponsored by a major university and featured well-known presenters from the research community and federal government. During a break, one of the participants commented that, although the content of the workshop was excellent, he was unsure what he could take back to his program. The double-blind studies and multivariate statistical analysis discussed had limited relevance to his needs, and his lack of a research background limited his understanding of the data. Since then, I have encountered this situation many times.

Chemical dependency treatment program administrators, board members, and staff want to know the impact their programs are having on their clients and the comparative quality of their services, but they may lack the skills and resources to do follow-up surveys. Furthermore, research designs common to academic researchers are often too expensive and unmanageable for a chemical dependency treatment setting. A simpler, methodologically sound way is needed for programs to do their follow-up evaluation. Also needed is greater sharing of data from more sophisticated studies.

A New Era

Chemical dependency treatment programs often go through cycles of external questioning and internal doubts. Today's era of cost containment results in new questions asked and old criticisms repeated. To maintain our service quality, we providers need to do a better job of evaluating. We also need to better understand other research results and know how to apply them to our programs. These are the purposes of this book—to enable treatment programs to do in-house outcome evaluations, and to better understand the findings of more complex studies done by the research community.

The first chapters of this book discuss the issues and methods of program evaluation. The later chapters include future trends and data from many research efforts encompassing a broad range of services. We conclude with a look at some case studies. But first, two authors, J. Clark

Laundergan and Patricia Owen, discuss the unique aspects of addictions research and chemical dependency research. The issues identified by these authors will help "set the stage" for the sections that follow.

PART I

SETTING THE STAGE

CHAPTER ONE

TREATMENT MODELS AND OUTCOME EVALUATION

J. Clark Laundergan, Ph.D.

J. Clark Laundergan has been active in chemical dependency research for over fifteen years, during which time he served as a research consultant with the Hazelden Foundation and the Miller-Dwan Medical Center in Duluth, Minnesota. He has been a faculty member in the Sociology-Anthropology Department at the University of Minnesota, Duluth, for more than twenty years. He recently completed a faculty exchange in Scandinavia where he studied alcoholism treatment.

DEFINING CHEMICAL DEPENDENCY

Our theories of the nature of chemical dependency directly affect treatment design and treatment outcome expectations. Thus,

- outcome evaluation is directed by treatment goals.
- treatment goals are defined by how we view alcoholism and other drug abuse.

So, exploring our view of the nature of chemical dependency is appropriate before questioning research and treatment outcomes.

Is chemical dependency a disease? If so, what are the characteristics of that disease? Or does chemical dependency not exist, but do individuals instead acquire learned behavior responses that result in symptomatic drinking? Is what we call chemical dependency the product of biochemical malfunction, and is it therefore best treated with chemotherapy? The answers to these questions have practical consequences for the researcher. As the authors of *Alcoholism and Treatment* state:

> The problem of how to define alcoholism constitutes more than an inconvenience or semantic debate. Rather, its definition has significant consequences for research, treatment, and public policy (Armor, Polich, and Stanbul 1976).

Researchers (Sugarman 1982; Ward 1983) suggest several models of alcoholism, including the following:

- the AA model
- the medical model
- the psychoanalytic model
- the behavioral model
- the social model (which I will discuss as the Minnesota Model)

Each of these models represents a different view of the nature of alcoholism, although they are not mutually exclusive; that is, proponents of the various models emphasize differing characteristics of the problem, but may incorporate some features of other models in their understanding of the nature of alcoholism.

THE ALCOHOLICS ANONYMOUS MODEL

E. M. Jellinek's work continues to influence contemporary understandings of alcoholism. In developing the concept *chronic alcoholism,* Jellinek introduced another important term, *loss of control,* or a person's inability to give up drinking even when desiring to do so (Bowman and Jellinek 1941). The term *loss of control* was later elaborated in Jellinek's detailing of the symptoms and the natural stages of alcoholism in an individual, resulting in what we know as the "Jellinek Chart" (Jellinek 1952). Loss of control is the symptom that differentiates symptomatic drinking from addictive drinking (i.e., dependency). The symptoms that Jellinek presents in the chart were identified in a survey of ninety-eight, and later, two thousand male members of AA. Not all alcoholics display all the symptoms nor are they necessarily exhibited in the order shown in the chart (Paredes 1976). Though Jellinek's early work is important in its own right, it became even more significant because much of his formulation became part of the concepts of the already developed Alcoholics Anonymous movement.

Alcoholics Anonymous considers alcoholism to be a disease of mind, body, and spirit with loss of control being its principal defining symptom. Regaining mental, physical, and spiritual health requires admitting powerlessness and turning one's will over to a Higher Power in order to begin recovery from this chronic disease—alcoholism. Continuing recovery necessitates working the Twelve Steps of AA within the fellowship of AA. Although the concept of alcoholism accepted by AA includes Jellinek's early scientifically based interpretations, the understanding of alcoholism that is current in AA is not a scientific formulation in the sense of traditional research-based theory.

Alcoholics Anonymous is unique in that it is treatment for alcoholism in its own right and is also an aftercare referral for other formal treatment efforts. Because AA is an anonymous fellowship of recovering alcoholics, the recovery progress of its members is not well documented, although the World Service Office of AA has approved some surveys of the membership. While a large portion of AA members receive treatment or counseling prior to coming to AA, there is considerable variation among AA groups (Maxwell 1982). The majority of members (52 percent) had no other intervention in their alcoholism other than attending AA meetings, according to a 1977 survey. But more and more people are accepting and turning to treatment and other assistance, both prior to affiliating themselves with AA and participating in AA.

Public opinion about AA is generally favorable and therefore its popular acceptance is independent of evaluation studies reporting treatment effectiveness. This public acceptance is not shared by many alcoholism researchers whose orientation demands empirical documentation of program outcome. "No valid claim to a success rate can be established for AA because no records are kept on how many alcoholics are exposed to AA only to go away and die unremitted or how many alcoholics who, after minimal exposure to AA, go away and recover" (Leach and Norris 1977). Although some in the scientific community remain skeptical, one clear advantage of AA as either treatment or post-treatment aftercare is that, as a voluntary fellowship, it is available without cost to the participants.

THE MEDICAL MODEL

Advocates of the medical model consider alcoholism to be a *disease* in the more biochemical sense of that term. Alcoholics are said to have constitutional liabilities, although the biological markers for identifying susceptibility to alcoholism have yet to be identified. Begleiter's research on brain deficits (1987, 1988) and work done on neuropsychological deficits (Tarter et al. 1984; Hegedus et al. 1984; Hill et al. 1987) are examples of studies directed at identifying biological markers. Genetic researchers conclude that alcoholism runs in families but have yet been unable to determine the extent or specifics of hereditary factors (Goodwin and Guze 1974).

Identification of biological markers represents a growing effort but shows inconclusive results.

The medical model has contributed to treatment of alcoholism by making available prescriptions of Antabuse, used as an alcohol inhibitor, and by treating physical complications resulting from heavy and prolonged use of alcohol.

Yet, there is no single comprehensive medical model of alcoholism treatment, so there is no clearly identified procedure for evaluating outcomes. Medical expertise is used to varying degrees in many treatment modalities. Hospital-based alcoholism treatment is more likely to use physicians as part of the treatment team than are free-standing nonmedical settings. In general, treatment programs rely on physicians for initial physical examinations and problem monitoring where there is minimal medical participation. Psychiatrists treating alcoholism may represent the medical model, the psychological model, or a combination, as well as being associated with the behavioral and Minnesota Models.

THE PSYCHOANALYTIC MODEL

Those who espouse the psychoanalytic perspective, view an individual's abuse of alcohol and problems resulting from the abuse as more symptoms than identifiable entities. They see repetitive heavy use of alcohol as evidence of a personality disorder and, accordingly, the treatment that is most often recommended is long-term individual or group psychotherapy. "The traditional psychoanalytic approach involves working backwards from the defences—repression, denial, and reactive grandiosity—to the underlying psychological conflicts" (Sugarman 1982). Individual therapists use traditional psychoanalysis as well as transactional analysis and gestalt therapy to bring about an awareness of suppressed psychological conflicts. While psychoanalytic treatment of alcoholism has had little systematic evaluation, psychoanalysis is generally seen as time consuming, costly, and unsuccessful in treating alcoholism (Ward 1983).

THE BEHAVIORAL MODEL

Those who treat alcoholism through behavior modification see alcohol use problems as learned behavior that can be modified. Positive and negative reinforcement direct learning and explain behavior. The alcoholic's behavior can be clinically modified by using positive or negative reinforcers to curtail or alter undesirable behavior and to develop new behaviors. Behavioral experts see people's alcoholism as being similar to other dysfunctional behaviors that are considered treatable through these techniques. Two treatment techniques of behavioral modification are

- aversion conditioning
- operant conditioning

An Aversion-Based Technique

One form of aversion conditioning has been used in a mainstream alcoholism treatment process that dates back to the 1930s at the Shadel Sanitarium in Seattle. It has been used at a number of treatment facilities operated as

Schick Shadel Hospitals and formerly through Raleigh Hills Hospitals. Clients develop an aversion to alcohol through use of the drug emetine along with drinking alcoholic beverages. Emetine is administered to clients who then look at alcohol, smell it, swish it in their mouth, and swallow it in small quantities before they develop nausea and vomiting caused by the emetine. The objective, that clients acquire a conditioned aversion to alcohol, is conducted in a peer-oriented treatment milieu where alcoholics can talk informally and interact with counselors who are alumni of the treatment.

An early study of treatment effectiveness reported 60 percent of over four thousand patients treated between 1935 and 1948 were abstinent for a one-year period (Lemere and Voegtlin 1950). More recent work by Cannon and his associates (1986) support the emetic alcohol-aversion therapy as proven effective with 45 percent of the sixty clients in the study who were abstinent at twelve months after treatment.

Other forms of aversion conditioning used in treating alcoholism are electrical shock and negative images. These techniques are used more experimentally than as a core therapy. Electrical shock is used much like emetine in the chemical aversion technique, or it is used to discourage the client from choosing alcoholic beverages over nonalcoholic beverages in a clinical setting. No evidence points to electrical shock as a superior means over chemical aversion in treatment of alcoholics (Miller and Barlow 1973; Cannon, Baker, and Wehl 1981). Associating negative images with drinking behavior is an aversive technique that lacks the discomforts of electrical shock and emetine; it has not been tried on large populations of alcoholics.

Experimenting with Another Variation

Operant conditioning emphasizes positive reinforcers but also uses techniques such as electrical shock with the emphasis on avoiding shocks. A well-known example of this therapy is the controversial work done at Patton State Hospital by Sobell and Sobell (Sobell 1978). The Sobells reject the idea that alcoholism is a single entity and that problem drinking behaviors are chronic. Using the tools of operant conditioning, they experimented by treating two groups with behavioral therapy and two groups with what they term *conventional treatment.*

Twenty subjects received behavioral treatment with the controlled drinking goal, and fifteen received this treatment with the abstinent goal. The operant conditioning was done in a simulated bar and cocktail lounge and in a simulated living room. Shock avoidance was used as was video taping and playback, and behavioral training consisting of role playing, role reversal, assertiveness training, and so forth.

The reported favorable outcome of this experimental treatment has been questioned by Pendery, Multzman, and West (1982) and defended by Marlatt (1983). Apart from the controlled drinking question that has generated part of the debate, operant conditioning used in treating alcoholics continues to be used primarily in small-scale experiments. Because it is of interest to behaviorally oriented psychologists, this form of treatment is inordinately profiled in this field's literature relative to the number of clients that it serves. Pattison and the Sobells (1977) link the multivariate model of alcoholism with behavioral treatment techniques in their book, *The Emerging Concept of Alcohol Dependence;* however, their anticipated widespread acceptance of this approach to alcoholism treatment did not occur in the 1980s. Nevertheless, evaluation outcome literature cites a greater number of studies considering controlled drinking outcomes than the availability of this treatment approach seems to warrant.

THE MINNESOTA MODEL

Alcoholism is an identifiable entity in the Minnesota Model:

> The symptoms common to alcoholism have been corroborated so that alcoholism may be identified by the person using alcohol in a stereotyped, repetitive, maladaptive fashion (Laundergan 1982).

Although individual drinking patterns and consequences vary, they are similar enough to identify the condition termed *alcoholism.* According to the Minnesota

Model, alcoholism is termed a *disease* in the same sense as are other medical-behavioral conditions such as eating disorders and emphysema. The disease alcoholism is identified by characteristics similar to those in Jellinek's chart of alcoholism progression:

- negative consequences associated with drinking alcohol
- preoccupation with drinking
- protecting the supply of alcohol
- use of alcohol to control physical and psychological feeling states
- solitary and rapid drinking
- increased tolerance and blackouts

Like the characteristics Jellinek identified, all these traits are not found in every alcoholic. For every alcoholic, however, recovery from chronic alcoholism requires abstinence from alcohol and changes in lifestyle. Recovery is therefore a lifelong process demanding much more than abstinence from alcohol or other mood-altering chemicals (Anderson 1981).

Intervening in the Disease

Within the Minnesota Model, treatment as conducted by professionals is intended to intervene in the active alcoholism by helping alcoholics recognize how alcohol has affected their lives, to encourage alcoholics to seek help, and to work with alcoholics to plan needed lifestyle changes and ways to implement the plan. The alcoholic becomes acquainted with the philosophy of Alcoholics Anonymous early on:

- The first five Steps of AA are used as the core of treatment.
- Bibliotherapy and group therapy familiarize patients with AA.
- Participation in AA is recommended in the aftercare plans of patients.

But treatment is more than a concentrated AA meeting. Patients are encouraged to understand that they must exercise personal responsibility and choice in their lives rather than accepting a role of victim. To help patients to this awareness, a variety of group and individual experiences promote self-awareness and personal insight. Treatment is intensive but of limited duration, so patients are expected to acquire the tools for continued introspection, assessment, and modification of unhealthy feelings and behaviors. For patients to improve their sociopsychological functioning, they will need to maintain abstinence from alcohol and other drugs. Abstinence is, therefore, both an end and a means to an end in the Minnesota Model of alcoholism treatment.

Achieving Worldwide Attention

Minnesota Model treatment serves large numbers of patients annually. Although more dominant in certain regions, it is used throughout the United States. In fact, the Minnesota Model is being used in other parts of the world. In Iceland, it is the dominant method of treatment. The Minnesota Model has also been introduced into Scandinavia and has attracted attention in Britain (Cook 1988).

Although highly visible and publicly popular as an effective treatment approach for alcoholism, the Minnesota Model is not associated with academic theories or an academic discipline. Consequently, it has not been the topic of much academic research. Some academics dismiss the Minnesota Model as being the same as AA.

Others simply ignore the Minnesota Model, as illustrated by Ward's omission of this model in his review of conceptions of alcoholism (Ward 1980). Only limited reporting of research on Minnesota Model treatment has been published in professional journals, in part because this treatment modality has not been academically popular. But another reason is that many working with the Minnesota Model have focused on quality assurance and outcome evaluation for in-house management use, rather than communicating to a wider professional audience reached through professional journals.

CURRENT LITERATURE

What patterns are found in the professional journal articles reporting alcoholism treatment evaluation studies? Thirty-one published alcoholism treatment evaluation studies (based on several treatment methods)* were identified using a computerized literature search.

Most programs served a mixture of voluntary and involuntary patients (53 percent) or voluntary patients only (28 percent). Only one program reported on an exclusively female population; the others reported on male-only patients (46 percent) and a mixture of males and females (43 percent). The average patient age for 68 percent of the studies was predominantly in the forty- to fifty-year-old range.

Most of the studies experienced attrition in their populations with one-fourth of the studies reporting a drop of between 16 percent and 30 percent from their initial sample. A total of 28 percent reported sample attritions greater than 31 percent. In approximately 22 percent of the studies, insufficient information was given about the loss of patients participating in the study during the study period. Loss of patients from the initial sample to the final sample could not be attributed to an unmanageably large number of patients being studied. Over half of the studies had less than one hundred patients in the final sample size, whereas only 15 percent reported on more than two hundred patients.

Most of the studies (56 percent) were done in the United States; most studied were inpatient programs, with outpatient programs represented at slightly less than one-third.

The profile of the thirty-one alcoholism treatment evaluation studies indicates some overall patterns, but considerable variability in patient and program characteristics.

Now to return to the central question of this chapter: what are the models and approaches of the programs being evaluated?

The conceptual frame of reference is most often not stated and must be inferred from the treatment mode and outcome criteria. Unfortunately, the treatment mode and evaluation

---

* These studies are indicated by the triangular symbol ▲ in the References on pages 14-18 at the end of this chapter.

criteria are not available in a large number of the studies. Further, one-third of the studies did not report length of treatment.

Most published research is of mixed experimental studies or variable treatment strategies with treatment lasting one to two months. Abstinence is the typical evaluation criteria and twelve-month post-treatment follow-ups are the the most frequent patterns in published research. The thirty-one studies were funded from a variety of sources but, once again, funding information was not given for many (44 percent) of the studies.

LOOKING FORWARD

If evaluation of chemical dependency treatment is to have meaning, researchers must clearly state the concept of chemical dependency, treatment mode, and outcome criteria. Then the studies may begin to address the effects of various theories of chemical dependency and treatment approaches. Currently, the literature, as represented by the thirty-one studies, restricts making meaningful statements about either theories of chemical dependency or program effectiveness because of the many studies providing inadequate information. How chemical dependency is defined, specifics on how it is treated, and clear criteria on how treatment is being evaluated need to be clear if studies evaluating treatment are to be more than a collection of unrelated statistics.

Minnesota Model alcoholism treatment program evaluation will need to become more evident in professional journals if it is to gain recognition as a viable treatment concept. Publishing evaluation studies on the Minnesota Model will contribute to the chemical dependency treatment outcome literature. But it may also be an opportunity to promote a standard for reporting complete information about the theories, treatment practices, and outcome criteria used in the programs being evaluated. Researchers and evaluators should accept the invitation to improve chemical dependency evaluation in these essential ways.

REFERENCES

Anderson, David J. *Perspectives on Treatment.* Center City, Minn.: Hazelden Educational Materials, 1981.

Armor, D.J., J.M. Polich, and H. B. Stanbul. *Alcoholism and Treatment.* Santa Monica, Calif.: The Rand Corporation, 1976.

Begleiter, H., and B. Porjesz. "Potential biological markers in individuals at high risk for developing alcoholism." *Alcoholism: Clinical and Experimental Research* 12 (1988): 488-93.

Begleiter, H. et al. "Auditory recovery functions and P3 in boys at high risk for alcoholism." *Alcohol* 4 (1987): 315-22.

Bowman, K.M., and E.M. Jellinek. "Alcohol addiction and chronic alcoholism." *Quarterly Journal of Studies on Alcohol* 2 (1941): 98-176.

▲Bullock, M. et al. "Acupuncture treatment of alcoholism recidivism: A pilot study." *Alcoholism* 11 (1987): 292-95.

Cannon, D.S. et al. "Alcohol-aversion therapy: Relations between strength of aversion and abstinence." *Journal of Consulting and Clinical Psychology* 54 (1986): 825-30.

Cannon, D.S., T.B. Baker, and C.K. Wehl. "Emetic and electric shock alcohol aversion therapy: Assessment of conditioning." *Journal of Consulting and Clinical Psychology* 49 (1981): 20-23.

Cook, C.C.H. "The Minnesota Model in the management of drug and alcohol dependency: Miracle, method or myth? Part I. The philosophy and the programme." *British Journal of Addiction* 83 (1988): 625-34.

Cook, C.C.H. "The Minnesota Model in the management of drug and alcohol dependency: Miracle, method or myth? Part II. Evidence and conclusion." *British Journal of Addiction* 83 (1988): 735-48.

▲Critchfield, G., and D. Eddy. "A confidence profile analysis of the effectiveness of Disulfiram in the treatment of chronic alcoholism." *Medical Care* 25 (1987): 566-75.

▲DeLeon, G. "Alcohol use among drug abusers: Treatment outcomes in a therapeutic community." *Alcoholism* 11 (1987): 430-36.

▲ Denotes reviewed studies.

DeSoto, C.B. et al. "Symptomatology in alcoholics at various stages of alcoholism." *Alcoholism: Clinical and Experimental Research* 9 (1985) 505-12.

▲Edwards, G. et al. "Normal drinking in recovered alcohol addicts." *British Journal of Addiction* 81 (1986): 27-37.

▲Elal-Lawrence, G., P. Slade, and M. Dewey. "Treatment and follow-up variables discriminating abstainers, controlled drinkers, and relapsers." *Journal of Studies on Alcohol* 48 (1987) 39-46.

▲Fawcett, J. et. al. "A double-blind, placebo-controlled trial of lithium carbonate therapy for alcoholism." *Archives of General Psychiatry* 44 (1987): 248-56.

▲Friedman, A., and N. Glickman. "Residential program characteristics for completion of treatment by adolescent drug abusers." *Journal of Nervous and Mental Disease* 175 (1987): 419-24.

▲Gilbert, F.S., and P.J. Maxwell. "Predicting attendance at follow-up evaluations in alcoholism treatment outcome research." *Journal of Studies on Alcohol* 48 (1987): 569-73.

Goodwin, D.W., and S.B. Guze. "Heredity and alcoholism." *The Biology of Alcoholism: Clinical Pathology.* Vol. 3, ed. B. Kissin and H. Begleiter. New York: Plenum Press, 1974.

Hegedus, A.M. et al. "Static ataxia: A possible marker for alcoholism." *Alcoholism: Clinical and Experimental Research* 11 (1984): 345-48.

Hill, S.Y. et al. "Static ataxia as a psychological marker for alcoholism." *Alcoholism: Clinical and Experimental Research* 11 (1987): 345-48.

▲Irwin, M. et al. "Use of laboratory tests to monitor heavy drinking by alcoholic men discharged from a treatment program." *American Journal of Psychiatry* 145 (1988): 595-99.

Jellinek, E.M. "Phases of alcohol addiction." *Quarterly Journal of Studies on Alcohol* 13 (1952): 673-84.

▲Kruzick, D. et al. "Alcoholism treatment outcome among career soldiers." *International Journal of Addictions* 21 (1986): 139-45.

Laundergan, J.C. *Easy Does It: Alcoholism Treatment Outcomes, Hazelden and the Minnesota Model.* Center City, Minn.: Hazelden Educational Materials, 1982.

Leach, G.B., and J.L. Norris. "Factors in the development of Alcoholics Anonymous (A.A.)." *The Biology of Alcoholism: Treatment and Rehabilitation of the Chronic Alcoholic.* Vol. 5, ed. B. Kissin and H. Begleiter. New York: Plenum Press, 1977.

Lemere, F., and W.L. Voegtlin. "An evaluation of the aversion treatment of alcoholism." *Quarterly Journal of Studies on Alcohol* 11 (1950): 199-204.

▲MacDonald, J.G. "Predictors of treatment outcome for alcoholic women." *International Journal of Addictions* 22 (1987): 235-48.

▲MacKenzie, A., R. Allen, and F. Funderburk. "Mortality and illness in male alcoholics: An eight-year follow-up." *International Journal of the Addictions* 21 (1986): 865-82.

MacKenzie, A., F. Funderburk, and R. Stefan. "The characteristics of alcoholics frequently lost to follow-up." *Journal of Studies on Alcohol* 48 (1987): 119-23.

Marlatt, G.A. "The controlled drinking controversy: A commentary." *American Psychologist* 38 (1983): 1097-1109.

Maxwell, M.A. "Alcoholics Anonymous." *Alcohol, Science, and Society Revisited* Ed., E.L. Gomberg, H.R. White, and J.A. Carpenter. Ann Arbor: University of Michigan Press, 1982.

Miller, P.M., and D.H. Barlow. "Behavorial approaches to the treatment of alcoholism." *Journal of Nervous and Mental Disease* 157 (1973): 10-20.

▲Mitchell, S., R. Page, and V. Morris. "Changes in treatment-related concepts of illicit drug abusers related to time in treatment in two residential treatment programs." *International Journal of Addictions* 22 (1987): 885-94.

▲Nace, E., J.J. Saxon, and N. Shore. "Borderline personality disorder and alcoholism treatment: A one-year follow-up study." *Journal of Studies on Alcohol* 47 (1986): 196-200.

▲Nordstrom, G., and M. Berglund. "A prospective study of successful long-term adjustment in alcohol dependence: Social drinking versus abstinence." *Journal of Studies on Alcohol* 48 (1987): 95-103.

▲Orford, J., and A. Keddie. "Abstinence or controlled drinking in clinical practice: A test of the dependence and persuasion hypothesis." *British Journal of Addiction* 81 (1986): 495-504.

Paredes, A. "The history of the concept of alcoholism." *Alcoholism: Interdisciplinary Approaches to an*

Enduring Problem. Ed., R.E. Tarter and A.A. Sugarman. Reading, Mass.: Addison-Wesley, 1976.

▲Parsons, O.A. "Cognitive functioning in sober social drinkers: A review and critique." *Journal of Studies on Alcohol* 47 (1986): 101-14.

Pattison, E.M. "A conceptual approach to alcoholism treatment goals." *Addictive Behavior* 1 (1976): 177-92.

Pattison, E.M., M.B. Sobell, and L.C. Sobell. *The Emerging Concepts of Alcohol Dependence.* New York: Springer, 1977.

Pendery, M.L., I.M. Multzman, and L.J, West. "Controlled drinking by alcoholics? New findings and reevaluation of a major affirmative study." *Science* 217 (1982): 169-75.

Pickens, R.W. et al. "Relapse of alcohol abusers." *Alcoholism: Clinical and Experimental Research* 9 (1985): 244-47.

▲Powell, B. et al. "The dropout in alcoholism research: A brief report." *International Journal of Addictions* 22 (1987): 283-87.

▲Rounsaville, B. et al. "Psychotherapy as a predictor of treatment outcome in alcoholics." *Archives of General Psychiatry* 44 (1987): 505-13.

Rush, B.R., and A.C. Ogborne. "Acceptability of nonabstinence treatment goals among alcoholism treatment programs." *Journal of Studies on Alcohol* 47 (1986): 146-50.

▲Sanchez-Craig, M., et al. "Cognitive-behavioral treatment for benzodiazepine dependence: A comparison of gradual vs. abrupt cessation of drug intake." *British Journal of Addiction* 82 (1987): 1317-27.

▲Sanchez-Craig, M., and H. Lei. "Disadvantages to imposing the goal of abstinence on problem drinkers: An empirical study." *British Journal of Addiction* 81 (1986): 505-12.

▲Schukitt, M.A., M.G. Schwei, and E. Gold. "Prediction of outcome in inpatient alcoholics." *Journal of Studies on Alcohol* 47 (1986): 151-55.

▲Sereny, G. et al. "Mandatory supervised Antabuse therapy in an outpatient alcoholism program: A pilot study." *Alcoholism: Clinical and Experimental Research* 10 (1986): 290-92.

▲Shore, J. "The Oregon experience with impaired physicians on probation: An eight-year follow-up." *Journal of the American Medical Association* 157 (1987): 2931-34.

▲Skutle, A., and G. Berg. "Training in controlled drinking for early-stage problem drinkers." *British Journal of Addiction* 82 (1987): 493-501.

▲Smith, D.I. "Evaluation of a residential AA program." *International Journal of Addictions* 21 (1986): 33-49.

Sobell, M.B., and L.C. Sobell. *Behavioral Treatment of Alcohol Problems.* New York: Plenum Press, 1978.

Sugarman, A.A. "Alcoholism: An overview of treatment models and methods." *Alcohol, Science, and Society Revisited.* Ed., E.L. Gomberg, H.R. White, and J.A. Carpenter. Ann Arbor, Mich.: University of Michigan Press, 1982.

Tarter, R.E., et al. "Adolescent sons of alcoholics: Neuropsychological and personality characteristics." *Alcoholism: Clinical and Experimental Research* 8 (1984): 216-22.

▲Taylor, C., et al. "Alcoholism and the patterning of outcome: A multivariate analysis." *British Journal of Addiction* 81 (1986): 815-23.

▲Thurstin, A., A. Alfano, and V. Nerviana. "The efficacy of AA attendance for aftercare of inpatient alcoholism: Some follow-up data." *International Journal of the Addictions* 22 (1987): 1083-90.

▲Verinis, J.S. "Characteristics of patients who continue with outpatient treatment." *International Journal of Addictions* 21 (1986): 25-31.

Ward, D.A. "Conceptions of the nature and treatment of alcoholism." *Alcoholism: Introduction to Theory and Treatment* 2d ed., rev., Ed., D.A. Ward. Dubuque, Iowa: Kendall/Hunt, 1983.

▲Watson, C. "Recidivism in 'controlled drinker' alcoholics: A longitudinal study." *Journal of Clinical Psychology* 43 (1987): 404-12.

▲Zweben, A. "Problem drinking and marital adjustment." *Journal of Studies on Alcohol* 47 (1986): 167-72.

CHAPTER TWO

CHEMICAL DEPENDENCY RESEARCH

Patricia Owen, Ph.D.

Patricia Owen is a licensed consulting psychologist and Vice President of Hazelden Services, Inc. Following Laundergan's general discussion, Owen focuses on the special issues related to addictions research.

Chemical dependency professionals know well the "cunning, baffling" nature of the disease. And the same characteristics that make chemical dependency difficult to recognize and treat also make the outcome of treatment difficult to measure. Those attempting to measure treatment outcome must grapple with some of the most elusive aspects of the disease.

THE COMPLEXITY OF DIAGNOSIS

There is no litmus test for chemical dependency. Pathognomonic signs do not show up on an X-ray, in a blood test, or in brain waves. While objective information aids in diagnosis, in the end the diagnosis depends almost entirely on a skilled clinician eliciting information from the patient. Additional reporting by friends and relatives can help, but these observations, like any "eye witness" information, are likely to be distorted or unavailable.

The difficulty of diagnosis affects measurement of treatment outcome in a variety of ways. Some people who are not truly addicted may be diagnosed as chemically dependent: for example, they may be in only a phase of heavy use. Although some are in the early stages of chemical dependency, others are going through only a finite period of inappropriate use. It is likely that those exceptions who control their use after treatment were misdiagnosed as addicted in the first place. Further, not all people coerced into treatment because of a legal infraction or positive urine screen are chemically dependent. And, oddly enough, others may over-report their alcohol or other drug use history. This can happen when a normal user finds himself or herself in an environment where everyone else is recovering. We occasionally find that among young people, some believe that claims of heavy, inappropriate use, "junkie pride," will help them fit in with admired peers.

Some clients who appear to be chemically dependent may actually have a primary psychological disorder. The question, "does he drink because he is crazy, or is he crazy because he drinks?" is not always answered accurately for some people in treatment.

THE NATURE AND INTENSITY OF TREATMENT VARY

While every path to chemical dependency leads to the same end point, treatment needs to be individualized. Unlike many medical disorders for which a physician can consult a reference book for the treatment protocol, no generic treatment plan works for chemical dependency. And as we learn more about the recovery process, related disorders, and other factors, treatment continues to evolve and become more complex. This variability in treatment approaches confounds our ability to correlate the treatment process with patient outcome.

THE SEGMENT OF POPULATION OR SAMPLE VARIES

The nature of the disease also guarantees that some people will drop out of treatment or that some people will be inappropriate for treatment. Out of hope or compassion, some people are admitted to treatment who may not belong there; they will leave or be discharged within the first few days. They may be cognitively or physically impaired and do not improve with abstinence, good food, and rest. Others have a concomitant mental disorder that unexpectedly surfaces. It may be so severe or beyond the skills of the treatment staff that the patient needs treatment in a psychiatric unit.

In other instances, a few people persist in denial of their disease beyond the early stages of treatment and, in fact, become more adamant. Their level of denial precludes them deriving any benefit from the treatment program. Finally, some may have emergencies, consequences of their disease, that prompt them to leave treatment. For example, family dissolution, court dates, or loss of business may interfere to the point that trying to keep a patient's mind on treatment is fruitless. (Treatment staff may consider these clients' inability to focus on treatment as another manifestation of denial.)

The question becomes, how should these people be counted in a treatment outcome study? Is it fair to leave them out of the outcome sample entirely, assuming that they have not really received treatment? Or, should they be counted as treatment failures?

DENIAL AND SELF-REPORT

After their treatment, some people who are asked about substance use will inaccurately deny having used again. No one likes to admit defeat. If the inquirer is a favorite counselor, patients may claim success to maintain the counselor's good regard or to avoid confrontation. Conversely, if the inquirer is someone unknown to the former patient, it may be easy to bluff through the interview.

Phrasing questions to precisely measure the course of the disease may be difficult. People may under- or over-report because each interpret differently the same question. For example, if two people who used codeine after a tooth extraction were asked, "Have you used a mood-altering substance since treatment?" one may answer yes, the other no. Refining the outcome questions to reflect every aspect of possible relapse may make the questionnaire or interview so long that patient cooperation decreases.

Some researchers use family members to collaborate with or represent the patient in a follow-up interview. Surprisingly, reports by significant others are about as accurate or inaccurate, depending on how you look at it, as patients' self-report. This is probably due to denial on the part of the family member, or perhaps the family member does not know. For example, patients in treatment commonly report that by the time they reached treatment, they had their families so confused that family members could not tell whether the chemically dependent person was sober or intoxicated.

HEALTHY MOVES AND GEOGRAPHICAL ESCAPES

A trait of the disease that complicates outcome research is that many patients move following treatment. For several, the move will be healthy and will be a sign of continued good progress. These people may leave an unhealthy family situation or peer group, or they may give up the job that makes them vulnerable to relapse. Conversely, some may end their estranged lifestyle and return hundreds of miles to their former home.

But for other people, the move may be a geographic escape. They may tell themselves that the reason they ended up in treatment was because everyone in their former environment thought any little use was bad. They may also tell themselves that once they live in a "better place," their problems won't seem so big and they won't need a drink. Or, perhaps they've had a relapse after treatment and got into enough trouble that others have asked them to live somewhere else.

Whatever the reason for clients' moves, no doubt the person doing outcome research will have difficulty tracking down the initial sample of treatment participants. Should those who cannot be found be counted as assumed relapsed, or should they be excluded from the sample entirely?

WHEN IS A SLIP A RELAPSE?

Just as the course of the disease is complex, so is the course of recovery. Two types of outcome are easy to categorize: those who use no mood-altering substances after treatment and, at the other extreme, those who use heavily, regularly, and inappropriately. But there is a third category: those who use briefly. For some, using after treatment has been their moment of truth: they needed to try it just one more time in an attempt to demonstrate that they could use like a nonaddicted person. But they discover that the evidence to the contrary supports everything they learned in treatment, and they quickly get back into their program. Should these folks be counted as treatment failures? Most would say not.

But where do we draw the line? After one slip? Two? A slip that lasts more than a day? A week? Common knowledge is that one slip can easily precede another until the time between slips decreases and the person is clearly off the wagon. Part of the nature of the disease is likelihood of relapse. Should a natural part of the disease be seen as a failure?

RECOVERY IS MORE THAN ABSTAINING

After treatment we expect more than abstinence. People who are in a solid recovery process generally report that all areas of their lives improve: relationships with family, friends, and Higher Power are better. They're thinking more clearly at work; attending AA; and making progress in working the Steps in their daily lives. While this may sound simple, it's difficult to measure. Let's look at some examples of this problem of measuring healthy sobriety.

On the one hand, you may have a woman who returns home from treatment to a demeaning and low-paying job, a belittling, actively alcoholic husband, two out-of-control teenagers, and a mother living with them who is stricken with Alzheimer's disease. The chemically dependent woman stays where she is because she believes she must—until her children are grown and her mother is no longer living or is in a nursing home. She maintains abstinence and has hopes for things changing in the future. But now that she is not seeing her situation through drug-clouded eyes, she admits to periods of emotional upset and despair, and reports a poor quality of life. She attends AA regularly, however, and has a sponsor.

On the other hand, there may be a woman who does not drink, but maintains abstinence more out of defiance than acceptance. She's angry, unhappy, and miserable to be around. She attends AA, but only because her husband said he'd leave her if she didn't follow her treatment plan.

She, like the woman previously described, reports abstinence and a poor quality of life.

Here are two people whose progression of disease after treatment has taken totally different turns. Most would consider the first a treatment success (albeit tenuously), and the second a treatment failure. Looking at the objective treatment data, however, each is abstinent, attending AA, and reporting a poor quality of life. There are undoubtedly many other scenarios with different combinations of AA attendance, quality of life indicators, and abstinence.

LEFTOVER CONSEQUENCES OF THE DISEASE

The world does not stop for a person who enters treatment. As consequences of the disease,

- the spouse and family may leave
- the business that was hanging by a thread may fold
- bankruptcy may become inevitable
- crimes committed may come to light
- courts may give sentences

A wealthy, married businessman with three kids, no criminal record, and an ostensibly good business may be, six months after treatment, bankrupt, deserted by family, living in a boarding house, and doing community service as restitution for checks that were forged prior to treatment. Anyone looking at his situation would say that his life became worse after treatment, when in fact it is the inevitable unfolding of the consequences of the disease. On a more complex level, this fellow (if recovery was going well for him), may describe himself as a treatment success, in that he stopped the lying and manipulation that kept his disease alive. He now may be abstaining, attending AA, and retaining close relationships with fellow AA members. Which brings us to the next point.

ANY MEASURE OF OUTCOME IS MERELY A SNAPSHOT

Any measure of outcome is merely a snapshot of an unfolding process of improvement or deterioration. In one instance, a person who is a stellar outcome of abstinence and AA involvement can totally unravel in one day. But in another instance, an abysmal failure, a person who has spiraled downward, returning to destructive use and reaping the consequences, can turn around in one day with what some call a conversion experience. Almost every seasoned recovering person knows this. For this reason, a *good outcome* is a collection of days passed with no substance used and earnest involvement in AA.

Although statistically, those who are sober at six months are likely to maintain longer-term sobriety, outcome is a day-by-day situation. This is why many prefer to use the adjective *recovering* rather *recovered*. One question for the outcome researcher is how far into recovery can a treatment center claim success, and when is the success more attributable to AA and other factors in the former patient's life?

PROGRESSING IN THE CONTINUUM OF CARE

Many people who leave primary treatment go to halfway houses, extended care units, very structured aftercare programs, psychiatric treatment, or prison. Some of these people, who are doing as well as their cohorts in terms of following the treatment plan, may not be the easiest to include in the outcome study. If a person has been in a structured setting during the entire outcome period, it is difficult to say he or she has had the same test of sobriety as those who are on their own. (Others might point out that mood-altering substances could be used in any setting, so the living situation shouldn't matter.) The point here, of course, is that part of the complexity of the disease is that the treatment of it really doesn't have a clear end point.

TO SUM UP

The characteristics of chemical dependency are not unique to it. Many of the same dilemmas posed by chemical dependency occur in outcome studies of most psychological disorders (such as depression, anxiety and, to some extent, even schizophrenia) as well as some physical disorders (for example, many types of chronic pain). *Success* in treating other chronic illnesses such as AIDS, cancer, or heart disease may be similar to many of the indicators of success in treating chemical dependency. We hope for remission for a significant period of time, ideally, to allow a normal life span and an improved quality of life. While these treatment goals are simply stated, their attainment and measurement is complex.

Part II is a step-by-step guide through the process of measuring this recovery process.

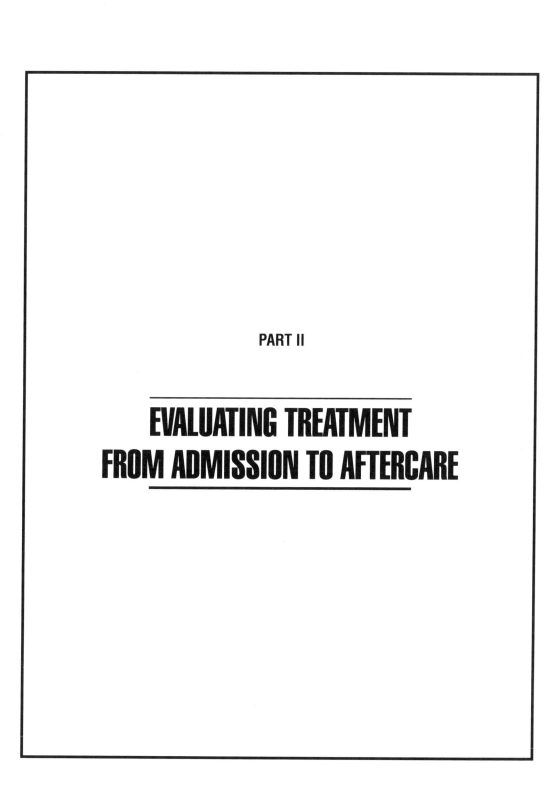

PART II

EVALUATING TREATMENT
FROM ADMISSION TO AFTERCARE

CHAPTER THREE

WHAT IS EVALUATION?

Jerry Spicer

> Evaluation research is the systematic collection of
> information about the activities and outcomes of actual
> programs in order for interested persons to make
> judgments about specific aspects of what the program is
> doing and affecting (Patton 1978).

This definition directs our attention to the two domains of
evaluation: what a treatment program does (process) and its
effects (outcomes). Furthermore, Patton stresses the need
for those conducting an evaluation to be concerned with providing information to facilitate decision making. Everybody
is an evaluator. We are all continually judging the efficiency
and effectiveness of our programs. Unfortunately, for many
of us, evaluation stays at an intuitive and subjective level.
In 1963, Pittman made a statement that is still relevant
today regarding alcoholism treatment programs:

> Perhaps the greatest weakness of all alcoholism
> treatment programs, whether in North America or Europe,
> is the lack of critical evaluation of their success or failure
> with alcoholic patients. Anecdotal material, patient
> material about how much they liked the facility, poems
> which patients write extolling the virtues of the programs
> and the staff, and clinical statements of physicians and
> psychiatrists about their success tell us little, if anything,
> about the success of the facility (Pittman 1963).

Although Pittman and others have noted that the chemical dependency treatment field lacks good empirical information about its programs, much progress has been made

since 1963. This section is written with the intention of helping people develop systematic, scientific techniques to demonstrate how well their treatment program operates and what long-term effects their program has. The focus is on evaluation as a management and planning tool. I believe that the persons reading these pages want information that can be used to improve their programs and ultimately benefit their clients.

WHY EVALUATE?

The field of chemical dependency treatment is increasingly under pressure to demonstrate outcomes and to be more accountable to funders and clients. This need to meet the accountability demands of various funders and standards and licensing groups is important to a program. There are other reasons for evaluation, but if the sole purpose of an evaluation is to provide data as a defense against criticisms by outsiders, the evaluation will probably be seen as a burden to the staff. The project will be viewed as a bureaucratic imposition of limited use to the program itself.

Perhaps a more important reason than providing information needed for accountability purposes is that evaluation data should facilitate decision making and planning; it should also be linked to quality assurance systems. Most of us are operating in a vacuum of information. We go along from day to day, often making decisions without enough information and hoping that the program will survive and the quality of treatment will be maintained. The information gained from an evaluation, however, can be systematically used to answer major questions.

Another purpose of an evaluation is to improve the program. Evaluation is useful in the development and improvement of a program because it provides data on program impact, efficiency, and the attainment of major program goals. Basically, an evaluation has three primary purposes:

- meeting accountability demands
- facilitating decision making and planning
- improving programs and services for clients

TYPES OF EVALUATION

Formative and Summative Approaches

Because there are many types of evaluation, a program must determine which approach is most appropriate to its needs. Programs interested in development or change should use what has been called formative evaluation. Formative studies are projects that are used to develop or improve a program. The audience in a formative study is the program staff, not an external body. These studies are often shorter and simpler projects that result in quick feedback. Internal staff should be involved in the study.

In contrast to a formative study, a summative evaluation is used to make an overall judgment about a program. Feedback and program change are not the major purposes of a summative study. "Did the program work?" or "What did the program do?" are summative questions. A summative study typically comes "after the fact" and is usually directed to the questions of external funders, boards, and other similar groups (and, less often, to internal staff questions). Often the study is done by outsiders, resulting in one major report.

Before proceeding with an evaluation, an initial decision is whether the study should be designed to provide timely and relevant data for program development (formative) or to make an overall judgment about the program (summative). Regardless of which approach is chosen, a study can emphasize either program processes (what was done) or outcomes (what the effects were).

Process Evaluation

Evaluation research often focuses on program processes or what was done. There are many options for studying the treatment process. The most common type of process evaluation study is the management information system (see Chapter Eight by Donald Jones and Kevin Johnson). Here, data are collected on the clients who enter treatment, including what happened to these people during treatment, and their discharge status. Information systems may be computerized and a monthly or quarterly report is generated, telling staff how much work they did over a specified period of time. The standards written by state licensing boards or the Joint Commission on the Accreditation of Healthcare Organizations are also process standards in that they specify what a program should do. Programs in a hospital setting may find that quality assurance audits are another way of studying the treatment process.

Outcome Evaluation

Determining the effects of the program on clients is outcome evaluation. In this case, the primary concern is the impact of the program on its clients. Treatment impact is typically measured through the follow-up survey. A follow-up survey can be either a one-shot summative evaluation that is externally sanctioned, or a formative study done by the program itself with ongoing feedback to the program. I will often emphasize formative evaluation, since I believe that evaluation research should contribute to program development and provide timely feedback for decision making. See figure 3.1.

EXAMPLES OF EVALUATION OPTIONS

	Formative Studies	Summative Studies
Process Focus	• Internal information system • Quality assurance • Patient satisfaction survey	• External governmental reporting system • Licensing; accreditation • Case review by funders
Outcome Focus	• Patient outcome • Customer/referent/community surveys • Cost-impact analysis	• External outcome studies done by funding agencies • Cost-benefit analysis

FIGURE 3.1

DIFFERENCES BETWEEN EVALUATION
AND BASIC RESEARCH

An ongoing debate in the field of evaluation is the difference between evaluation and basic research. Undoubtedly, this discussion is primarily a concern of evaluators and researchers, and the reader may have little interest in this topic. There are, however, some distinctions between evaluation and research that the beginning evaluator should consider when designing a study.

Research is commonly defined as the use of scientific techniques to test and build theory. The audience for research is often the research community, and the goals are to accumulate knowledge and test general principles.

The evaluator often has more immediate interests than the researcher. The evaluator is likely to be interested in studying specific questions relevant to a program, but of limited applicability for the larger research community. The differences between evaluation and research are more a matter of degree than having distinct characteristics. Figure 3.2 presents a continuum with simple reporting and review mechanisms at the low end of scientific rigor, program evaluation being in the middle position. The goal in a patient follow-up study is to strike a balance between scientific rigor: and practicality. The study design must meet the basics of good research, while reflecting the reality of limited resources.

SCIENTIFIC METHODS

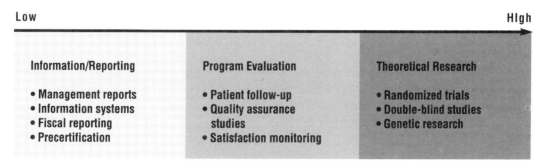

FIGURE 3.2
EVALUATION/RESEARCH CONTINUUM

LINKING EVALUATION TO PLANNING AND MANAGEMENT

Although evaluation is less concerned with theory building, it should be seen as a means of collecting empirical information to aid in program management.

> Evaluation is primarily a process within on-going organizational management, decision-making, and planning; and it is only secondarily a research enterprise for the purpose of new scientific discoveries (Attkisson et al. 1978).

This quotation emphasizes that evaluation is a continuous process that should be linked to management and planning. For optimal effectiveness, the evaluator will be a staff person with access to those persons (administrators, board, funders) responsible for making decisions about the program. Outcome studies should be combined with other forms of evaluation to gain a comprehensive view of program operation and outcomes. To maximize the effectiveness of evaluation, reports should be timely and address important programmatic issues. Further, even though this book supports the need for internal evaluation, evaluators should maintain their independence and consciously recognize their own biases. Finally, periodic external review of a program and the evaluation system should be an integral part of the overall evaluation plan.

LIMITATIONS AND ADVANTAGES OF FOLLOW-UP SURVEYS

All of us are in an ongoing process of evaluating or making judgments about our programs, and we have many reasons for our interest in program evaluation. We may wish to meet accountability demands or plan and deliver better services. Additionally, many of us have a natural curiosity about the nature of treatment and its outcome. The non-researcher can use evaluation to answer some significant questions about program outcomes and the impact of treatment on patients' lives.

Limitations of Follow-up Surveys

A question often raised in discussions of evaluation is, "What are the advantages and disadvantages of follow-up surveys?" The person considering follow-up treatment evaluation should recognize that a follow-up survey is not going to prove that a program is a success. Later in the book we will return to this issue, but we should emphasize here that success can have many meanings. Also, no program is ever successful with all its clients.

Another problem with a follow-up survey is that it typically takes one and one-half to two years before the data are available. A twelve-month follow-up survey means that the first questionnaires will not be mailed until one year following clients' discharge. Therefore, the final report will not be available until eighteen to twenty-four months after the clients' treatment. There must be enough program stability that the data that are available in two years will remain relevant to program needs.

The necessity for some program stability in order to relate data on former clients to current questions does not mean that the program should not change. But major and unplanned swings in program philosophy may limit an evaluation's usefulness. A more significant issue related to the long turn-around time for a follow-up survey is that of accountability. Once a client leaves treatment, the program no longer has a direct influence on him or her. Nonetheless, treatment programs are held accountable after treatment for how well their clients are doing. Client outcome reports should note that outcomes at twelve months reflect not only treatment effects, but also succeeding events in the patient's life over which the program often has little control.

As discussed earlier, a follow-up survey is not process oriented. A follow-up survey can, at best, partially measure process by using client satisfaction scales. Some researchers refer to a follow-up study as a *black box design* (O'Briant and Lennard 1973). That is, treatment is a "black box" and evaluators measure what happens to people after treatment without trying to understand the treatment process. But if a program has a good management information system and/or a quality assurance function, the outcome data can be correlated with information on the treatment processes. Finally, there are measurement problems in conducting follow-up surveys. These problems will be discussed later; it should be noted that they are not unique to chemical dependency treatment, but are common to any survey research.

Advantages

With these limitations in mind, the follow-up survey can still do much for a program.

- First, a follow-up survey results in objective outcome data demonstrating program effectiveness and provides information for program development and planning. Thus, a follow-up survey can help meet accountability demands.
- Second—and this is often overlooked—a follow-up survey supports program continuity. The survey cannot be accomplished without a focus on long-term planning. Many of us tend to look six months down the road, but follow-up research requires planning for two to three years. This can have some major benefits. In planning for a long-term follow-up study, staff develop a feeling of continuity and stability; they may be less likely to alter a program until outcome data are available.
- Third, once the data begin to come in, staff are receiving feedback on their work for the first time. Staff morale may improve as they see the impact they are having on their clients' lives. Patient outcome data can also be linked to quality assurance and marketing research information.
- Finally, a follow-up survey provides a system for aftercare contact and client self-assessment. Sending a questionnaire will not suffice as an aftercare program, but the questionnaires can maintain post-treatment contact with clients and establish a means of client feedback.

Several times a week, we receive letters from patients who received a questionnaire and are seeking additional assistance or want to thank Hazelden for all the help they received. As a result of the follow-up system, the staff in our program can directly affect clients by responding to these letters. Staff reviews the returned questionnaires and if the former client is having problems, an additional follow-up contact is made. This feedback, although often informal and subjective, can be rewarding to both the evaluator and the counselor. An example of comments a former client wrote on a one-year follow-up survey is this:

> I appreciate the questionnaires—they help me to stop and look at myself and my progress. You are helping me to stay sober even a year after my discharge. I don't know of any other treatment center that regularly continues follow-up contact. The questionnaires make me feel like I belong to something and that someone is interested in me and cares. I don't feel like just another drunk who has been sent through the "wringer" and then forgotten.

CHAPTER FOUR

THE PLANNING STAGES

Jerry Spicer

The preceding chapter noted the importance of having a stable program before undertaking an evaluation. Other issues to consider in determining readiness for evaluation are the following:

1. Are those administrating the program able and interested in undertaking a follow-up evaluation at this time?
2. Is there support for evaluation from the staff, board, and funders?
3. Are there sufficient resources in terms of time, money, and expertise?

If these prerequisites are lacking, the evaluation planning stages will take more time as stability, interest, support, and resources are developed.

THE INITIAL PLANNING

To develop a follow-up evaluation, it is common for one staff person to draft a questionnaire that is approved by some of the key staff. It is then launched with little discussion among other people connected with the program. Under these circumstances, the study is apt to encounter resistance and fail to be successfully completed. Therefore, it is crucial that the planning of an evaluation system be done carefully and involve those people who will be affected by the study.

- *It is necessary to list all the people who are important in developing the follow-up evaluation model.* For example, staff, administration, your board, the secretary responsible for sending out the forms, a consultant or expert, and former clients would all be useful on an evaluation planning committee. If the report is going to be used to meet some accountability demands, every effort should be made to ensure that funders and/or local coordinating bodies are included in the planning process. Allow people the opportunity to voice their criticisms and concerns before the project is begun. This will help prevent hindrances later.

- *The first task of the group's planning should be to determine the most important unanswered questions.* Do not start by designing the questionnaire, developing a budget, or determining the sample size. Bring the planning group together and ask them to list information about the program that is important to them (Patton 1978). Allow them to list as many significant issues and areas of uncertainty as they can. Do not limit the questions to the issue of treatment outcomes.

- *Next, summarize the group's comments.* Some important programmatic informational needs may be addressed without developing a follow-up survey. When I have done this exercise, I typically find many questions concerning such issues as length of stay, program completion rates, referral sources, types of problems at admission, and so on. Answers to these questions can be found in patient records. These questions do not need to be the focus of a follow-up survey, but belong in your data collection and information system or in your ongoing administrative or management reporting systems.

Outcome questions pertaining to program effectiveness should be listed and prioritized in significance to the program. From this list, a follow-up methodology and questionnaire can be designed. Start simply by meeting the major needs of the program.

The important objective in introducing evaluation is not to see how much can be undertaken, but how much of what is done is relevant (Attkisson et al. 1978).

More specific and expansive studies can be developed later. Remember that in a year, you are going to be inundated with questionnaires and data. Unless you specify and limit the information you need, you will likely be overwhelmed and find it impossible to complete the data analysis and reports.

In particular, be cautious about the often strong emphasis among many evaluators in measuring program goals. Be careful in studying stated program goals. Goals set for programs may have been designed more to please a funder than to indicate what is actually being done. Program goals are more often statements of philosophy and wishful thinking than of realistic outcome expectations. Goals may be vague and unmeasurable. There may also be many program effects that cannot be summarized in a series of goal statements (Salasin 1974). The question "What do *you* want to know?" should determine your evaluation design, rather than a design that measures only program goals.

BUDGETING FOR A FOLLOW-UP SURVEY

Early in the development of your evaluation model there will be questions concerning budget. Budgets for a follow-up survey include the usual costs for personnel, materials, and fees, but there are some unusual aspects of a follow-up study budget. The most important principle to remember is that the cost for a follow-up survey of all clients will be low in the first year, will increase in the second year, and will stabilize in the third year.

Figures 4.1 and 4.2 show an example breakdown of cost for a one-year follow-up.

In the first year, most of the costs are developmental. The expenses associated with planning, the use of consultants, and perhaps some travel costs will be in the first-year budget. Also, during this time, there may be some minor expenses for printing of questionnaires, setting up data processing procedures, and acquiring the initial report on the pre-test. The first year will be devoted to getting the follow-up system underway; and in the second year, the actual mailing of the questionnaires to the previous year's clients begins. Therefore, year two's costs will be greater and will include the costs for mailing and processing of questionnaires.

Does Your Program Measure Up?

Cost	Year One (1988)	Year Two (1989)	Year Three (1990)
1. Development costs: • planning • consultants • travel • material • printing		No development costs	May be minor costs for revisions
2. Mailing and processing of questionnaires, materials and printing	Minor costs to set up procedures and for pre-testing instruments	For 1988 clients	For last of 1988 clients For first returns from 1989 clients
3. Data processing and analysis	Minor costs to set up procedures and for pre-test	Some for first returns from 1988 clients	For 1988 clients For first returns from 1989 clients
4. Report writing	Minor costs for report on pre-test	Minor costs for initial reports	Report on 1988 clients

FIGURE 4.1

BUDGETING FOR A ONE-YEAR FOLLOW-UP SURVEY

By the third year, the mailing and processing of questionnaires from clients dating from year one will be underway as well as the first mailing to year two clients. This means that in year three, the budget includes finalizing of the follow-up of year one clients, the mailing for year two clients, and the first reports coming out of the follow-up for the year one clients. A follow-up budget should include adequate funding for data processing, analysis, and writing of the reports. Data processing and report writing will occur in the late part of the second year or first part of the third year. Therefore, funding should be adequate for at least two and one-half years, but preferably for three.

A cost-saving option is to survey a sample of clients. An easy sampling method is to study all discharges for a several month period. For example, all clients discharged in January, February, and March would be sent questionnaires. This approach also has the advantage of complet-

AGENCY: _____   TIME SPAN: ___12 Months_____

PROJECT NAME: _Outcome Evaluation Study_   CONTACT PERSON: _____
        1, 6 and 12 month questionnaires.
        Supplemental phone contact

SAMPLE SIZE:___600 (60% response rate)___

	Subtotal	Total
1. Personnel		$28,000
Administrative (25% of Director's time)	$ 8,000	
Clerical		
Follow-up data clerk (full-time)	$16,000	
Telephone interviewer (quarter-time)	$ 4,000	
2. Travel		$ 2,000
3. Materials and printing		$ 2,500
4. Training (staff workshops)		$ 500
5. Equipment		$13,800
Telephone	$ 800	
Computer software and associated costs	$ 1,000	
Office equipment	$ 2,000	
Personal computer	$10,000	
6. Consultant fees		$ 2,500
7. Miscellaneous costs (postage)		$ 1,200
	Subtotal	$50,500
8. Indirect costs-30% of above		$15,150
TOTAL COSTS	**Total**	**$65,650**

FIGURE 4.2
SAMPLE BUDGET - THIRD YEAR
(for follow-up project already implemented)

ing the study sooner, the last questionnaire being sent one year after March. But if the follow-up survey is designed to serve an aftercare function, you will want to attempt to contact all clients who were treated. Any sampling method may introduce bias into the study and the sample should be representative of the entire patient population (see Chapter Five for a discussion of sampling).

Some hints for follow-up study budgeting follow:

- Reduce the cost of a follow-up study by spreading it over several fiscal years. Start a follow-up study midway through one fiscal year, then spread the cost over two fiscal years.
- The number of questionnaires mailed to clients will directly affect the cost of the project. Obviously, it costs more to send five hundred questionnaires than it does to send one hundred. And it costs more to send two questionnaires (for example, at six and twelve months) to each client than to send them each one.
- In telephoning clients, anticipate making three or more attempts before completing the interview.
- Budget for duplicate mailings, special surveys, and supplemental telephone follow-ups.
- Try to include the costs for evaluation as part of clients' treatment fees. In our experience, programs that allocate $90-$100 per client for evaluation will have enough funds for ongoing follow-up surveys. A reasonable position here can be that evaluation is a regular part of the treatment process and should be funded as such. A one-shot summative study would be less expensive.
- Using volunteers can reduce costs (this can also increase community awareness and support of the program).

In the next chapter, we will discuss steps for developing a follow-up system. After completing these steps, the items to be included in the budget will be easier to identify.

CHAPTER FIVE

THE FOLLOW-UP SYSTEM

Jerry Spicer

Early in the planning and discussion of a follow-up evaluation, you should review other studies and reports on outcome evaluation and research. This review may be brief but will orient you to previous findings and key variables to measure. On pages 210–211 is a Bibliography that lists some well-known studies in this area.

PROCEDURES

Gathering Data Begins During Treatment

Before clients can be mailed a questionnaire, interviewed, or contacted by telephone, a program needs basic documentation on them. At the time of admission, the client's name, address, a secondary contact source (preferably a family member), as well as necessary background information, should be collected. It is important that the follow-up data be logically linked to the types of information collected during treatment. Figure 5.1 gives a rough breakdown of some of the documentation that could be collected on clients during treatment.

It is important that these data be collected and coded in a like manner to the information collected at follow-up. Therefore, questions on chemical use and social and psychological functioning should be similarly phrased at both admission and follow-up to provide a measure of change over time. It is vital that accurate addresses, telephone numbers, and secondary contacts be collected at admission and *verified* with clients before they leave treatment. A useful option is to ask the clients to give their forwarding addresses and secondary contacts on the follow-up permission forms that they sign when they are discharged.

DOCUMENTATION

I. At Intake
  A. Client code or number
  B. Identification data —name, address, telephone number, next of kin, etcetera
  C. Referral and immediate treatment history
  D. Major presenting problems or special needs
  E. Demographics —age, sex, etcetera
  F. Administrative and financial data
  G. Release forms
 	
II. Medical History
 	
III. Assessment Data
  A. Chemical use
  B. Treatment history
  C. Demographic and socioeconomic
  D. Psychological and mental health status
  E. Family and social situation
  F. Legal problems, residental status, recreational activities, spirituality
 	
IV. Process Documentation
  A. Individualized, problem-orientation recording
    1. Definition of the problems
    2. Assessment and plan
    3. Services provided for all problems
    4. Change and/or resolution levels
 	
  B. Services provided
 	
V. At Discharge
  A. Permission form for follow-up contact
  B. Address
  C. Significant other's name and address

FIGURE 5.1

Determining Length of Follow-Up

The planning group must decide how long to follow clients and how frequently to contact them during the follow-up period. A one-year follow-up is most commonly accepted. Hazelden has found little change in client outcomes, as a group, between six, twelve, and eighteen months. In fact, it has been reported (Davies 1956; Pattison 1968) that 90 percent of the clients who return to drinking or other drug use do so within the first three months after leaving treatment. Still, many people feel more comfortable with the longer follow-up period of one year. Nonetheless, it is important to maintain some type of contact with the client between the time of discharge and the time of the one-year questionnaire.

I recommend a telephone call, letter, or postcard at some point or points between discharge and one year as a means of keeping in contact with clients. The discharge date should be the starting point for the follow-up process, in order to control for length of treatment. Clients in open-ended programs or aftercare programs will receive questionnaires while they are still in treatment unless they are followed after discharge.

Weighing the Methods of a Survey

There are four options for collecting data from clients at follow-up:

1. mailing questionnaires
2. telephone interviews
3. personal interviews
4. a combination of all these

The mailed questionnaire requires the least staff time and collects similar information from all clients. A rule of thumb for a mail questionnaire is that it require no more than half an hour for the client to complete. Fifteen to twenty minutes is even better. Many people are reluctant to return questionnaires, and those people who do not return your questionnaire should be telephoned.

Although the telephone interview can be used to gather data from people who did not respond to a mailed questionnaire, many will wish to terminate the interview before completion. It is recommended that the most important data be collected first. The telephone interview is useful when the sample is small and the questionnaire is brief. In this case, telephoning may be even less expensive than mailing. (See the Bibliography on page 209 for references on surveying techniques.)

The personal interview, though useful for gathering in-depth data, is also more expensive because an interviewer must be hired to contact the clients. Yet clients with limited education and reading ability are more amenable to telephone or personal interviews than to mailed questionnaires.

PUTTING THE PARTS TOGETHER IN YOUR RESEARCH DESIGN

To obtain the data you need, a sound research design is required. The research design should have three components. First, try to collect information on clients at more than one point in time. The standard method is to use pre-treatment and post-treatment measures. The pre-treatment data typically documents the client's behavior patterns for the year preceding treatment. This information can be collected at admission to the program. At one year after treatment, the post-treatment data measures behavior in the twelve months since treatment. Comparing the pre- and post-tests gives a measure of change.

The second part of a good research design is a comparison group. As will be discussed in Chapter Six, a "control" (patients not receiving treatment) group may violate our treatment standards. An attempt should be made, however, to compare data, for example, between people who complete treatment and those who do not, or between younger and older clients. Making comparisons gives you a better understanding of the diversity within the sample and can also indicate which groups are most improved after treatment and which show the greatest change over time.

Finally, question the clients about their use of other services (other treatment, AA) since discharge. In addition to the effects of your treatment program, patients' recovery is greatly impacted by events in their lives shortly following discharge and their participation in aftercare, AA, or other such programs.

Setting the Sample Size

In any type of survey, some people will not respond to your questionnaire. Because of this loss of data, it is recommended that as many clients as possible be contacted unless you have a very large agency. For research purposes, a sample of one hundred may be sufficient for data analysis. But mailing one hundred questionnaires may result in a return of only sixty-five. Also, to compare groups the sample will be divided. For example, if there are one hundred returns and males and females are compared, then the two samples might be seventy males and thirty females, both groups being too small for further analysis. Surveying only thirty females limits the data analysis and a larger initial sample should have been collected.

An alternative to following all clients or a random sample of several hundred is to select certain key groups for follow-up. Those clients of particular interest to the agency, such as a certain age group, can be surveyed. One of the simpler sampling techniques is to follow all clients admitted in a certain time period, say over a four-month period. This may not, however, be a true random sample.

Maintaining an Adequate Response Rate

As questionnaires are mailed, it will be become evident which groups of people are least likely to respond. You will need to make special efforts to contact them. Individuals who do not complete the treatment program may be unlikely to return questionnaires. Your agency may want to consider not contacting these people. But, if this option is chosen, the decision should be supported by the planning committee. You can take the stance that the main interest is with people who complete treatment. Excluding dropouts means that your outcome data will be explanatory *only* for people who complete the program. Another option is to exclude clients staying less than a certain number of days, since these people will not have received much treatment.

There are other ways of increasing the number of responses. I cannot stress too strongly the need for the treatment staff's support for the follow-up surveys. When counselors emphasize the importance of follow-up and the confidentiality of the data, the patients will be receptive to the evaluation. Personalize the follow-up system by sending letters to the patients and giving them the name of someone at your agency they can contact if they have any questions. Send a letter of introduction to patients during treatment and again at the time of discharge, explaining the follow-up system. At some point after their discharge, another letter should be sent, again explaining the entire system and requesting change of address information. Once the questionnaires are sent, wait a couple of weeks and then send another questionnaire and/or telephone those people not responding. In Hazelden's experience, the short telephone interview has been found to be most useful in increasing the response rate.

Designing a Questionnaire

Questionnaire design could constitute an entire book in itself. (See the "Questionnaire Development" Bibliography on page 212 for selected references.) Consultants can be helpful in developing questionnaires. Examples of the instruments used at Hazelden are included in Appendix B on pages 193–205. Studying them for ideas and format may be useful to you in designing your own. They were, however, designed to meet Hazelden's needs, so you will need to tailor your questionnaires to your program's needs.*

Several points concerning the design of questionnaires apply to follow-up surveys. First of all, remember that the questionnaire will be sent to various types of people. Efforts should be made so that the questionnaire is interpreted in the same way by all persons reading the questions. It is recommended that a questionnaire be divided into major sections, with the most important questions placed at the beginning. Because many people will not complete the entire questionnaire, asking the most important questions first will increase the information you receive. Provide adequate explanation on how to complete the questionnaire. Finally, have the questionnaire printed legibly and attractively. See Figure 5.2 for examples of problems you may encounter in developing a questionnaire.

What to Ask at Follow-Up

Figure 5.3 presents areas that should be included in an outcome survey. Obviously, the former clients should be asked about their present pattern of alcohol and other drug

---

* Forms and questionnaires in this book may be adapted for your use.

WORDING OF QUESTIONS

SOME SUGGESTIONS FOR THE WORDING OF QUESTIONS FOLLOW:

1. Avoid open-ended questions. Allowing people to write in their answers creates problems in summarizing the results and means that someone has to read all the responses and try to find patterns. Use closed-ended questions whenever possible.

   Example: an open-ended question...
   What is your present occupation?

   _____

   could be a closed-ended question...

   Please indicate your present occupation:
   _____ professional/managerial
   _____ technical
   _____ unemployed etc.

2. Allow a full range of options, including a chance to choose an "other" or "does not apply" answer.

   Example:
   How would you rate your present marital situation:
   _____ excellent
   _____ good
   _____ fair
   _____ poor
   _____ does not apply (for the single person)

   To whom do you turn for help?
   _____ relative
   _____ friend
   _____ clergy
   _____ does not apply (please explain)

3. Avoid overlapping categories.

   Example: (these choices overlap)
   What is your age?
   ____ 25 or under   ____ 25-35
   ____ 35-45   ____ 45 or older
   should be

   ____ 24 or under   ____ 25-34
   ____ 35-44   ____ 45 or older

4. Avoid words that may influence a response.

   Example:
   Your counselor stressed the importance of attending AA after treatment. Are you attending AA?
   __ Yes __ No
   should be

   How frequently are you attending AA?
   _____ once or twice a week
   _____ several times a week
   _____ not attending

5. Every question should contain only one idea to be answered with one response.

   Example:
   Are you drinking more than before treatment, less than before, or about the same?
   should be

   _____ no drinking since treatment
   _____ drinking, but less than before treatment
   _____ drinking about as much as before treatment
   _____ drinking more than before treatment

6. The responses should be appropriate to the question.

   Example:
   How helpful were the group therapy sessions?
   __ excellent __ good __ fair __ poor
   should be

   How helpful were the group therapy sessions?
   _____ very helpful
   _____ somewhat helpful
   _____ not very helpful
   _____ not helpful at all

7. Provide explanations throughout the questionnaire. Tell people when to choose only one answer, or to choose as many as apply, when to go to the next page, etc. Explain all unusual terms.

FIGURE 5.2

Does Your Program Measure Up?

FOLLOW-UP AREAS

I.   Chemical Dependency
    A. Problem at time of admission (alcohol, drugs, or both)
    B. Drinking patterns
       1. Abstinence and length of abstinence
       2. Quantity and frequency of use
    C. Use of other drugs
       1. Mood-altering drugs
       2. Medically prescribed drugs
       3. Over-the-counter drugs
       4. Caffeine, nicotine
    D. If using alcohol and other drugs, related problems
       1. Sleep, nutrition
       2. Memory lapses
       3. Shakes
       4. Quarrels
       5. Job
       6. Arrests
       7. Hospitalizations

II. Social Background
    A. Family status and functioning
    B. Employment

III. Treatment History and Support
    A. Additional treatment, services since discharge
    B. AA participation
    C. Other support - friends, family

IV. Maturation and Growth (client's self-perceptions)
    A. Relationship with family, friends, Higher Power
    B. Ability to accomplish tasks, give and accept help and advice, handle problems, manage finances, assume responsibility
    C. Health, job, self-image, recreational, sexual satisfaction

V.   Client Satisfaction (client rating of the program's services)
VI. Comments, Requests for Help, Change of Address

FIGURE 5.3

use. How much, how long, and how often they have been drinking should be determined. Distinguish between medically prescribed and non-prescribed drug use. A question on drug use at time of admission can be a reliability check (this will be discussed further in Chapter Six).

If there are usable data on drug use at admission, ask similar questions at follow-up. Comparing responses between these two time slots will give a measure of change. If there are no reliable admission data, then the respondents can indicate how their drug use has changed. Ask about other problems the person is having and ask if these are related to drug use.

Information on how frequently the former client is attending AA and other support groups is needed to understand the recovery process. Also ask if the person has used any other treatment or aftercare programs.

Hazelden has always asked a series of questions on psychosocial development (listed as "Maturation and Growth" in figure 5.3). These items allow the individual to indicate his or her perception of improvement in areas other than chemical use. Questions asking for an evaluation of treatment services ("Client Satisfaction" in the figure) are helpful in program planning and process evaluation. Finally, allow the respondent a place to comment, make suggestions, or request help. And *always* ask for a current address.

Coding and Using Technology

Set up questions in such a way that they can be manually or computer coded by assigning a number to each answer. Figure 5.4 is an illustration of ways to code data. As much as is possible, eliminate open-ended responses, and give each question's answers a numbering code. If a question has more than nine possible answers use two digits, beginning with ten.

Computers can frequently be used in data analysis. Meeting with knowledgeable people at a local computer center can help you develop your questionnaire. You will not need a computer programmer to write programs for the analysis of your data. A computer program, the *Statistical Package for Social Sciences,* can be found in college bookstores. This package will be sufficient for most types of data analysis. You will need to contract for computer time and assistance.

Does Your Program Measure Up?

(Do Not Write In This Space)
Column*

1-3   Client Number <u>0</u> <u>0</u> <u>1</u>

  4   1. Which choice best describes your present drinking level compared to before treatment?
          (*Choose one*)

            <u>X</u> (1) have not used alcohol since treatment
            ____ (2) drinking, but less than before treatment
            ____ (3) drinking about the same as before treatment
            ____ (4) drinking more than before treatment

      2. Which of these have been helpful to you since leaving treatment?
          (*Choose as many as apply*)

  5   <u>X</u> Alcoholics Anonymous/Al-Anon/Alateen
  6   <u>X</u> family member
  7   ____ clergy
  8   ____ none
  9   <u>X</u> other-please explain: _____ <u>neighbor</u> _____

10,11 3. How many months have you been in your present job? <u>18</u>

          *These column numbers are sometimes put on a questionnaire to facilitate coding. They correspond to the column numbers below.

Example - Coding System for Above

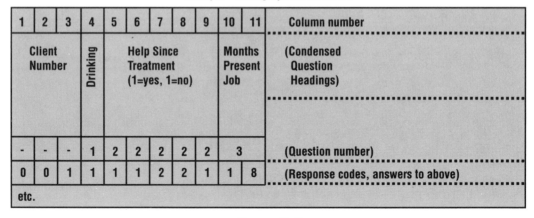

1	2	3	4	5	6	7	8	9	10	11	Column number
Client Number			Drinking	Help Since Treatment (1=yes, 1=no)					Months Present Job		(Condensed Question Headings)
-	-	-	1	2	2	2	2	2	3		(Question number)
0	0	1	1	1	1	2	2	1	1	8	(Response codes, answers to above)
etc.											

FIGURE 5.4
SAMPLE FOLLOW-UP SURVEY CODING SYSTEM

(based on possible answers)

Coding Pre-Treatment Data

The data collected at admission can also be coded to facilitate manual or computer analysis. Appendix B contains an "Abstracting Form" on page 193, developed by Hazelden for another treatment program. Every variable on the Abstracting Form is numbered and has either a closed-ended response to be checked or a set number of spaces (lines) to be filled in. Figure 5.4 is a form that is also capable of being entered directly into a computer or manually tabulated. In this case, the numbers in the small boxes that are aligned with the words, *column number,* designate the computer card column for keypunching.

Both of these forms summarize key variables collected at admission, during treatment, and at discharge. These data can be easily converted into monthly management reports describing the clients, length of stay, discharge status, and other essential information. Some of these questions can also be asked at follow-up (worded in the same way) to measure change. Write an instruction manual to explain the proper method of completing the forms.

ANALYZING DATA

You may need a consultant for data analysis and statistical presentation. The evaluation plan should include money and time for the analysis of the information and the writing of the report. Many of us have acquired a great deal of information that was never used because of lack of statistical expertise and money to hire an analyst.

It is important to remember that the basic purpose of statistics is to summarize large amounts of information. A follow-up questionnaire will contain many pieces of information about each client. Summarizing, presenting, and interpreting all the data necessitate statistical techniques. An audience that is not sophisticated in the use of statistics should not be presented with complex statistics. Know the audience and present the data in a way they can understand.

There are two basic kinds of statistics: descriptive and inferential.

Does Your Program Measure Up?

- *Descriptive statistics* are percentages, frequencies, and graphic ways of presenting data. Descriptive statistics do just what the term implies: that is, they describe the data.
- *Inferential or inductive statistics* permit assumptions to be made about the nature of the information presented. Knowing if the data are "statistically significant" can be important. That is, if the outcomes of two different groups are dissimilar, are the differences great enough to be real statistical differences or are the differences merely the result of random fluctuation?

A statistician can provide ways to determine the extent of differences between groups and the magnitude of that difference. More recently, people have been using correlational analysis to understand the nature of the relationship of different variables. A correlational analysis measures how strongly related different variables are.

Presenting and Interpreting Data

There are several options for reporting statistical information. Probably the simplest method is to summarize the information with percentages. Table 5.1 is an example of how data on attendance at AA can be displayed. In prepar-

TABLE 5.1

PRESENT AA ATTENDANCE

12 MONTHS AFTER TREATMENT

Frequency	N*	%
Once a week or more	52	49%
Once a week	33	31%
2-3 times a month	6	6%
Once a month	5	5%
Not attending	10	9%
Total	**106**	**100%**

* Number of responses

ing this type of table, precisely define the information in the heading. Also, include the actual number of responses ("N" for number, or "F" for frequency) to indicate the sample size and distribution of the data.

Table 5.2 shows another means of summarizing information. In this example, clients evaluated treatment services (client satisfaction) according to three degrees of helpfulness: much help, some help, and little or no help.

TABLE 5.2
HELPFULNESS OF SERVICES
ONE YEAR AFTER TREATMENT

	Rating %			
Service	Much Help	Some Help	Little or No Help	N*
Meetings with counselors	80	14	6	99
Informal patient conversations	71	23	6	99
Group therapy	71	20	9	98
Peer confrontation	54	22	24	97
Time alone	50	35	15	94
Meditation	48	28	24	92
Reading	45	44	11	98

* Number of responses

Because many clients did not use a service or did not answer a question, the number of clients rating each service varies. Thus, it is important to indicate the number (N) of clients responding to each question.

Comparing two groups is often called a *cross-tabulation*, and table 5.3 demonstrates the importance of completing treatment at Hazelden. The differences between those who have completed treatment and those who have not appear large in table 5.3. But in any research, differences among groups due to group size and random chance will always be

Does Your Program Measure Up?

TABLE 5.3
COMPARISON OF SUSTAINED ABSTINENCE*RATES
FOR REGULAR AND NONREGULAR DISCHARGES

	Persons Who Completed Treatment	Persons Who Have Not Completed Treatment
Sustained Abstinence*	61%	38%
Used Alcohol Since Treatment	39%	62%
N	777	68

* Sustained abstinence means the respondent has not used alcohol since leaving treatment.

apparent. As mentioned earlier, a significance test can be used to measure the magnitude of difference in the findings.

A simple significance test is called a chi-square.* Calculating a chi-square for table 5.3 results in a value indicating that 1 out of 1,000 times the difference between those who have completed treatment and those who have not would be due to random chance. Stated differently, the odds are that there is a real difference between people who complete treatment and those who do not, in their use of alcohol one year after discharge. The chi-square would have been expressed as $p<001$, (p meaning probability).

Sometimes we want to know how strongly related two variables are. An appropriate statistic to be used here is called a *correlation*. If there is perfect correlation, the score is 1.00, but most correlations are much less than that. For example, to test the validity of the follow-up data, a comparison of client responses with their significant other's responses on similar questionnaires can be made, as in table 5.4. The high correlations between patients and their significant others shows the validity of the follow-up data and is re-confirmed by the high percentages of agreement in the same table.

---

* *Webster's Ninth New Collegiate Dictionary* defines a chi-square as follows: "A statistic that is a sum of the terms each of which is a quotient obtained by dividing the square of the difference between the observed and theoretical values of a quantity by the theoretical value."

TABLE 5.4
PATIENT AND SIGNIFICANT OTHER RESPONSES
TO SIMILAR QUESTIONS AT 8 MONTHS AFTER TREATMENT*

Items	% of Agreement	Pearson Correlation
Problem at time of treatment	88	.76
Frequency of present drinking	86	.83
Quantity of present drinking	93	.77
Longest period of no drinking	86	.87

* Taken from *Hospital-Based Chemical Dependency Treatment: A Model for Outcome Evaluation,* Hazelden Educational Materials.

A number of errors can be made in using statistics. First of all, statistics do not *prove* anything about the data. Simply because variables are correlated does not mean that they have caused one another, and just because the data are statistically significant does not prove a theory is necessarily accurate on why the data are different. What statistics do is determine the probability that the findings are the result of error or random fluctuations and indicate the strength and direction of relationships among the data.

Be careful of assuming that group data can give information on individuals. If the outcomes on drinking behavior one year after treatment indicate that 50 percent of the clients are sober, that does not mean that each client is sober 50 percent of the time. Group data are based on *averaging* the responses of various individuals and do not accurately reflect any one person's status.

A final point is to be cautious in the ways that data are presented. Figure 5.5 shows two different ways of presenting some data from Hazelden. By changing the vertical axis the results look very different. A principle to remember is to use the same types of tables, graphs, and other displays throughout the report to make the report easier to read and to allow comparisons.

Statistical analysis can be important in *understanding* the accuracy of the data and interpreting the findings. A consultant would be needed in this area if no staff member has the necessary skills.

Does Your Program Measure Up?

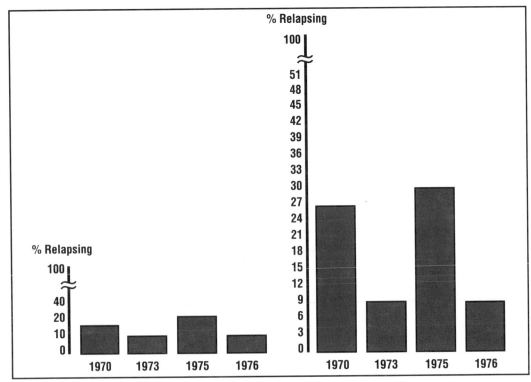

Figure 5.5
Patients Not Improved

These two sets of bar graphs demonstrate how the same data can be presented differently to give different messages. By extending the vertical axis in the right-hand set of bar graphs, the relapse rate appears to vary widely by year. Yet, the same data in the left-hand set, with a shorter vertical axis, gives the impression of only a modest variation in annual relapse rates.

Reporting

When you write a report, keep in mind to whom the report will be addressed. Know the audience and their level of sophistication. Assume that they will *not* read the report in its entirety. I advise using highlighting and summaries for major findings and points. Many readers skim a report, looking at the tables and then reading the introduction and the summary. Anticipate this in writing reports. Early in the development of evaluation design, plan for a verbal summary of the report for key people.

The final written report should include a brief overview of the type of program and clients involved. Following that, explain how the data were collected, and then give the results in the next major section.

Finally, it is not sufficient to write an annual evaluation report. Work with the planning group to design a series of brief and simple monthly or quarterly reports that provide information for those involved in the program. Once a year is too limited a payoff for people who have put a lot of effort into the evaluation.

PRE-TESTING

A pre-test is the final step once the research design and procedures are determined. The pre-test is important in helping to detect problems in the questionnaire or procedures. A handy rule of thumb is to give the first draft of the questionnaire to people of lower education than your sample. If this group can understand your questions, then your sample can probably understand the questions. The final pre-test should include sending questionnaires or interviewing at least fifty clients. The pre-test would include mailing questionnaires, computer coding data, and writing a sample report. Once the pre-testing is done, the budget can be finalized and the evaluation system can be initiated.

Remember the importance of the pre-testing, and once you begin, do not make major modifications in the questionnaire until the first major report is done. Any change limits your ability to compare results over several years. In the next chapter, I'll discuss special problems that might be encountered in a follow-up survey.

CHAPTER SIX

ADDRESSING SPECIAL ISSUES

Jerry Spicer

CHOOSING A CONSULTANT

Consultants can be helpful in evaluation research because of their expertise and their objective viewpoint. To find a consultant, you may want to contact local universities or federal and state agencies. Training and consultation in evaluation are also available at Hazelden and elsewhere.

Because of their objectivity, consultants can help with such issues as questionnaire design, as well as establish credibility for your project. If possible, have someone outside your agency write your major report. As a result, people reading the report may be more comfortable with the data and less likely to feel that there was a bias in the findings.

There are various options to finding a consultant. A consultant may be found who is willing to provide free help either as a community service effort or because he or she is a member of your board or in some way connected with your program.

As a means of paying a consultant, you may arrange for a fee-for-service method. This approach is easy to administer, and the consultant is paid upon completion of specified duties. Another way is to have a long-term contract with the consultant. This is appropriate if the consultant will be involved throughout the project. No matter what type of financial arrangement you negotiate, look for someone who has proven experience, skill, ethics, and understanding of the chemical dependency treatment field. Furthermore, the consultant should have access to resources such as computer technology and a library.

Spell Out Your Expectations

In the contract or fee-for-service arrangement with the consultant, precisely specify your mutual expectations.

Determine in advance the style of the report.

- Is the report to be written for a scientific audience or for a lay audience?
- How long should the report be, and how many revisions will the consultant make?

Such questions should be asked in any type of financial arrangement.

A potentially troublesome issue is the right of release and publication. Once the study is done, does the consultant have the right to release the report, or is the report confidential and the property of the agency? A further obligation expected from a consultant includes his or her willingness to make a verbal presentation of the data to the staff and the board. Another may be training staff in research techniques. There is no set fee for a consultant, and the rates will vary widely from person to person and from program to program. Again, I recommend that consultants be used in the areas of research design, data analysis, and to help prepare a final report.

METHODOLOGICAL ISSUES

An important methodological issue in doing a follow-up study is demonstrating the reliability and validity of the information. Reliability refers to the consistency of responses from the sample. Validity refers to whether the questionnaire measures what it is supposed to measure.

Measuring Reliability

Some people assume that survey data are not reliable, particularly when the respondents are chemically dependent persons. This has not been found true at Hazelden (Patton 1978) or by other researchers (Miller et al. 1979).

The reliability of responses can be measured by comparing answers both within a questionnaire and on subsequent questionnaires. For example, if a person indicates that the *frequency* of his or her drinking is "never," then on a question concerning the *quantity* of drinking, the person should say "none." Include reliability checks in the questionnaire, and then in the final report indicate how reliable the responses were. In addition, when a person is contacted more than once, repeat the previously asked question at the second contact, and compare responses in order to measure the reliability of information. At six months ask, "What was your problem when you entered treatment?" Then ask again at twelve months and compare the answers for consistency. Of course, this technique cannot be used with questions that could change from one time to another, such as present drinking behavior.

Checking Validity

One way to check the validity of the information is to send a similar questionnaire to a significant other or another person who can confirm the information. By asking the client's spouse or friend the same questions asked of the client, the responses can be compared and any major discrepancies noted. Permission must be given by the client to contact these other people.

Encountering Sampling Problems

A third area covers the issue of how representative the data are. Factors that will bias the data are sampling loss and missing data. Because some people do not respond, and some questions are not completely answered, data will not be available on everybody in the program. Furthermore, certain people may be excluded from the study.

Once the follow-up information is back, compare the types of people who returned your questionnaires with those who were originally sent questionnaires. Groups of individuals who did not respond should be noted in the report. The report should also indicate that there are not adequate data on those people.

Another issue is whether people who do not respond should be assumed to be treatment "failures." For example, around 5 percent of the sample will refuse to participate. The question becomes whether to treat these individuals as treatment failures, treatment successes, or to make no judgments upon them one way or another. It has been our preference at Hazelden to simply exclude from the data analysis those who refuse to respond. But some researchers assert that people who refuse to respond or who do not return questionnaires should be considered treatment failures. Hazelden's experience indicates that this is not necessarily the case, but we agree that the non-respondent is more likely to be doing poorly than the person who responds. As a result, follow-up data will be more favorably biased in terms of treatment outcomes.

ETHICAL ISSUES

Using Control Groups

A major ethical issue is the use of control groups. The experimental research design compares control and experimental groups. In this design, one group of people receives some type of intervention and is called the experimental group while another group receives no treatment and is called a control group. These two groups' outcomes are compared at some point following treatment of the experimental group. There is, however, a serious ethical problem in denying treatment to people for the purpose of research design. Further, the use of control groups in follow-up evaluation designs runs counter to program philosophy. This issue needs to be discussed in the initial planning stages of an evaluation design.

Another means of measuring treatment outcomes is to collect follow-up data and increase the size of the sample through time, then making comparisons among different groups. Use of a control group may become less important than comparisons, for example, between males and females, young and old, or those who have completed treatment and those who have not.

Notification and the Hawthorne Effect

In addition to the use of control groups, there are other ethical issues regarding follow-up evaluation. For example, should the clients be told that they are being studied? It is important for both ethical and legal reasons that clients be notified of the follow-up system and that they sign a release form, particularly if significant others are to be contacted. In the field of human research, a phenomenon called the *Hawthorne Effect* asserts that people change their behavior because they are being studied. Clients may alter the way they behave when they know that they are being followed and will receive questionnaires or be interviewed about their behavior. Yet, if a follow-up survey results in more improvement for the clients, the evaluator should accept this and be pleased with it. In a somewhat related initiative, Hazelden contacts clients who indicate on their questionnaires that they are having problems. If this contact is effective, we have interfered with our research design, but it is our conscious decision to do so.

Confidentiality and Right of Refusal

Never identify the person as having received chemical dependency treatment. Do not use words or addresses indicating that the survey is sent by a treatment program. Hazelden has used the term, *Continuation Program* to describe our survey and uses envelopes that are returned to a post office box. In telephoning, client confidentiality should also be maintained.

Be prepared for clients to refuse to participate in the study. Take all steps necessary to collect as much data as possible, but don't harass clients in order to collect more information.

Are You Prepared for Aftercare Issues?

Finally, at the time clients are contacted after discharge, there will be requests for some type of intervention or help. If, at twelve months from the time of discharge, you receive a letter with a questionnaire that says, "I need help," are you prepared and legally allowed or obligated to provide that support? We can assure you that these types of letters will occur, and your program will need procedures and policies for dealing with the requests.

DIFFICULT POPULATIONS: YOU MAY NEED ADDITIONAL SOURCES

For those programs having predominantly transient clients, young clients, and clients of low educational level, a follow-up evaluation system may be difficult to implement. An option for acquiring follow-up data with these types of people is to use two or three different confirming or secondary sources, such as relatives or other records. A likely criticism with this method concerns the reliability and validity of the information. It is, therefore, important to collect confirming and secondary data from as many sources as possible and to compare the data to check the accuracy. As mentioned earlier, our and other researchers' experience shows that significant others are generally accurate in evaluating the client's situation. Secondary sources are unlikely, however, to be able to respond to specific questions, such as number of drinks the client consumes per day. They are usually able to answer simpler questions such as whether the person is drinking or not.

OVERCOMING STAFF RESISTANCE: STRESS THE GOOD

Your staff may be resistant and anxious about evaluation. Clinical staff may resent the extra work and question the relevancy of the study. Even administrators, who are likely aware of the need for evaluation, may yet be unsure of the study. These staff have special characteristics that the evaluator should take into account (Schulberg and Jerrell 1979):

- Staff concerns are often with the immediate and relevant. Long-term studies may be seen as having limited usefulness.
- Program staff may rely more on meetings, discussions, and verbal feedback than on written reports.
- While the researcher may assume a skeptical, change-oriented role, the program staff often stress stability and the status quo.
- People who are not researchers may not understand the importance of research design, program stability, and measurement techniques.

There are many discussions about increasing the ability of evaluational research (Patton 1978; Davis and Salasin 1975; Milcarek and Struening 1975; Schulberg and Jerrell 1979). These viewpoints can be summarized as follows:

- To be useful, evaluation must address the questions of the program's key decision makers.
- An evaluation should be designed by several interested people. A study should not be forced or *sprung* on staff and clients.
- Feedback is important. A major report should be timely and relevant. A late report may end up being ignored. Short and quick feedback is important. Verbal presentations are necessary.
- Be pragmatic in judging evaluation. One study will not be the only information used in decision making, but it will be helpful.
- Reports that present only negative findings will be threatening and probably ignored. Provide solutions and alternatives for program deficiencies. Also stress the good accomplished and note positive program outcomes. Allow staff to review and comment on preliminary drafts of the reports.

DEFINING SUCCESS:
A PHILOSOPHICAL AND PLANNING ISSUE

Those who initiate a follow-up system to determine whether their program is a success will be frustrated. Success for a program is not a simple issue that can be presented in one or two statistical tables. What success means for a program is a major philosophical and planning issue. One of the common mistakes in the area of defining treatment success is to use only the abstinent/not abstinent criteria. Repeatedly, researchers have found that, although drinking can be an accurate indicator of program outcome, not all clients who are abstinent are doing well in other areas of their lives (Pattison 1963).

In determining program success, emphasize other changes in life as well as changes in drinking behavior.

Conversely, some people show improvement even though they are not abstinent. Following is a letter from one of our former clients who did not achieve Hazelden's goal of abstinence, but who shows improvement in both attitudes toward chemical dependency and willingness to accept help.

Does Your Program Measure Up?

Dear Jerry:

I apologize for the delay in replying to your questionnaire and my inability to complete it at this time.

On _____, eight days short of a year of sobriety, I took several drinks. Other than anxiety there were no immediate disastrous results. I remained dry about two weeks. Then, on _____, while engaged in an important professional project, I started drinking again. I controlled this sufficiently to continue to work for three days, but on _____, I drank excessively and that night my family and AA sponsor took me to the treatment unit at _____. The following week I resigned the position I have held for the past _____ years. A public announcement was made that I had resigned and was undergoing treatment for alcoholism.

I resigned for two reasons (in addition to my assumption that the company for which I have worked _____ years expected it). They were (1) I had promised after my last treatment that, if it happened again, I would resign; (2) I concluded that this job was an impediment to my successful recovery.

I completed a twenty-eight-day treatment program at _____. In the month since then, I have been at home, going to counseling three times a week, and attending from five to seven AA meetings a week. For the first time, my wife is also undergoing therapy.

My company has kept me on the payroll until the first of the year, pending completion of outpatient treatment. The company has offered me an opportunity to return in another capacity. I am weighing this against some other alternatives, including that of early retirement. My decision, with the help of counselors, will be made on the basis that my first priorities are sobriety and strengthening relations with my wife.

My renewed hope for successful recovery is based on these new factors which did not exist following my previous treatments: I am rid of the old job; I am undertaking a more intensive aftercare program than before; I have established more open, honest communications with my wife than before; and my wife is actively involved in therapy with me.

This relapse and treatment at a different facility have confused the questionnaire. However, I'd be happy to continue to cooperate with you in any way I can. I still have deep affection for Hazelden.

Sincerely yours,

_____

In the long run, such a person will probably be able to reach the treatment goal of abstinence, although he was still undergoing major lifestyle fluctuations. In determining program success, emphasize other changes in a client's life as well as changes in drinking behavior.

Finally, rely on clients' reports of improvement as a measure of your program's impact. Researchers and evaluators often establish their own criteria of success or improvement and force the client to meet those standards. One patient may report that her family life has shown major improvements, although she is still having problems in other areas. Success is relative to the program and the clients. Arbitrary measures of program success and simplistic comparisons with other programs are naive and, in the long run, frustrating tactics to take.

At this time, the field of chemical dependency treatment is under increasing pressure to demonstrate success to a variety of groups. Rather than reacting to this pressure, perhaps we should assume an educator's role and demonstrate to the public the need for services, the complexities of measuring program impact, and the complicated decisions to be made concerning human lives.

EVALUATION IS ONE SPOKE
IN THE WHEEL OF YOUR PROGRAM

A follow-up evaluation system is not a panacea for any treatment program. Evaluation should be seen as one part of a well-organized and well-run treatment program. As Schulberg and Jerrell say (1979), "Program evaluation thus has come to be viewed as an integral component of managerial functions and responsibilities."

Evaluation can be many things to different people. Consequently, programs should use a variety of evaluation techniques to meet the needs of different groups interested in improving the program. A follow-up survey should be part of a comprehensive evaluation system that includes process and outcome studies, along with measures of program quality. By systematically collecting follow-up data, the impact of chemical dependency treatment can be demonstrated.

An evaluator is expected to play the roles of researcher, administrator, and educator. Budgets and questionnaires must be written, data analyzed, and reports written. Because no individual can be all things to all people, the implementation of a follow-up survey should include other people. An evaluation team can combine their strengths and thereby enhance the study.

In undertaking a follow-up survey, be persistent, be patient, and design a system that will become a stable and integrated part of your program. Although there may be frustrations, the long-term benefits to your program and clients will outweigh the initial difficulties.

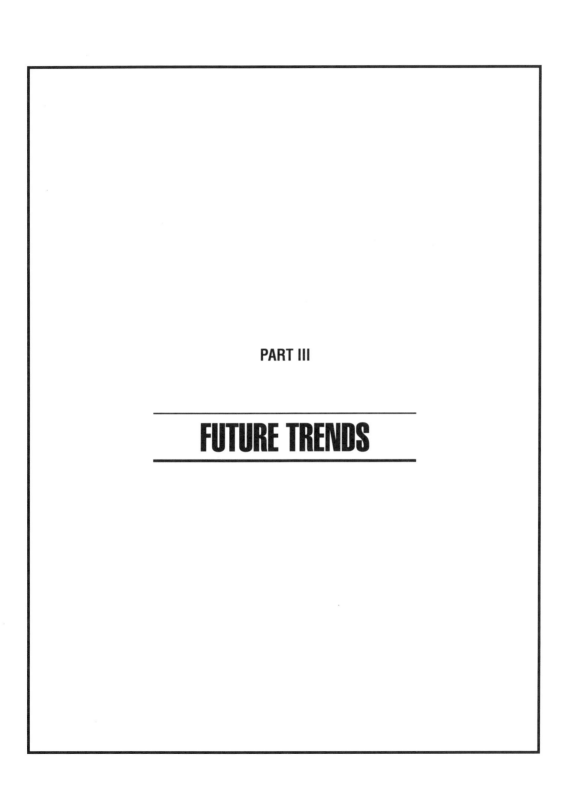

PART III

FUTURE TRENDS

CHAPTER SEVEN

LINKING QUALITY ASSURANCE AND OUTCOME EVALUATION

Jerry Spicer

Historically, quality assurance has focused on the treatment process, utilizing clinical peers to develop standards and review practice. External review by accreditation agencies was supported as a means of assuring uniform quality of care and that acceptable professional practices were used by accredited providers and individual professionals. Quality assurance, in contrast to outcome evaluation, has emphasized current services, peer review, less rigorous research designs, and demonstrable programmatic changes resulting from the study.

> Quality assurance of clinical care is designed to identify and correct deficiencies in services provided to patients. Quality review is typically accomplished by comparing care provided with professionally developed criteria that specify appropriate treatment for particular illnesses or behavioral problem areas. Clinical care that does not conform to professionally developed criteria [is] referred to a committee of peers for review and intervention through appropriate educational and/or corrective action (Attkisson et al. 1978).

Recent developments in external standards, however, show an expectation that patient follow-up data be included in the quality assurance system. There will be a twofold effect of this changing expectation: first, outcome evaluation systems will need to include data and reporting mechanisms that can be used for quality assurance and, conversely, quality assurance processes and staff will need to become more informed users of post-treatment data.

Outcome evaluation systems must begin collecting more data on the treatment process, including patient satisfaction, length of stay/treatment cost, and evaluation of treatment components. And outcome systems must be modified to collect and report data from periods closer to treatment discharge. Two-year-old outcome data is less relevant to quality assurance than information collected at discharge or a few weeks later.

Quality assurance staff and committees must become more comfortable with aggregate, rather than individual or case data, and use direct interviews with patients, rather than medical record information. They must know how to handle sampling loss issues and determine how to respond to complaints from patients no longer in treatment. An unresolved issue is the level of accountability a clinician or program may have with a problem encountered by a patient who was discharged several weeks earlier. A related trend in quality assurance and external standards is to extend the service provider's accountability to include aftercare services.

Though, historically, quality assurance and patient outcome systems have been separate activities, the future shows an increasing trend toward, at least, merging information at defined points. On the whole, this is a positive trend as quality assurance staff become more aware of longer term recovery issues, and as patient follow-up researchers see the relationship between service quality and treatment effectiveness.

CHAPTER EIGHT

INFORMATION MANAGEMENT IN THE CHEMICAL DEPENDENCY TREATMENT FIELD

Donald Jones and Kevin Johnson

Donald Jones is Director of Information Services for Ramsey County Human Services, St. Paul, Minnesota. Kevin Johnson directs Hazelden's Information Services.

Improved management of patient and program information can produce substantial benefits for chemical dependency treatment programs. Most providers, like other health and human service agencies, have a collection of fragmented, overlapping, and redundant reporting systems that were developed piecemeal. Yet, we recognize the need to manage information, just as we manage human and financial resources.

More efficient data management can streamline reporting to external groups, such as accreditation bodies, licensors, payors, and referents. More effective systems can help improve program management, including staff supervision, program monitoring, and marketing.

But the application of computer technology to a treatment program is not without its risks. Technology, particularly software development, can be expensive. Once developed, computer-based information systems often take on a life of their own, a sort of "creeping elegance," as one observer noted. And, after it is installed, a management information system can have many unanticipated and unintended impacts on a treatment center.

The goal of this chapter is to help program administrators improve the management information systems (MIS) operating in their programs while they also avoid some of the pitfalls involved in MIS design and implementation.

Definition of Management Information System

What exactly is a management information system? Perhaps the simplest answer is that it is information packaged for decision making. Let's examine those terms.

- *Information.* Most program managers already suffer from information overload—their daily inbox is filled with correspondence, memos, messages, printouts, and reports. And it is too easy to become jaded with too much information. Therefore, we need to distinguish between meaningful information (essential for program management) and data (facts we may find interesting, but that are not critical for us to know about). Before computerizing any system, we should ask ourselves some simple questions: So what? Do we really need this piece of information? Is it worth the money spent in collecting, storing, retrieving, and regularly reporting on it? And is it worth asking of all our patients?

- *Packaged.* People tend to ignore information that is not presented in a format that is comfortable for them. Graphics, for example, communicate better to some people than lengthy tables. Good packaging also requires that information in a report be accurate, timely, relevant to the user, and systematic.

- *For Decision Making.* The ultimate goal of an MIS is to guide management's decision making. With better information, treatment directors may learn more about their patients and staff and the efficiency and effectiveness of their programs. This new information should, in turn, lead to program improvements. For example, treatment centers often experience problems in their admissions office, resulting in waiting lists and lower patient census. An effective admissions MIS should help reveal the source of the problems (for example, inappropriate staffing levels, inefficient admissions procedures, inadequate telephone systems, changes in treatment coverage), so that a manager can make the needed adjustments.

In other words, an MIS should be decision-centered rather than data-centered. Program managers need to ask themselves what pieces of information are critical to carrying out their jobs. We remember delivering a lengthy patient follow-up report to one treatment director. He quickly leafed through the report to find the percentage of patients reporting sobriety at twelve months after discharge. Satisfied, he said, "My job is to keep the outcomes good and the beds full." That director certainly knew what his job was, and he knew the information (census and outcomes) he needed to measure his performance.

Not All Management Information Systems Are the Same

The term *management information system* is broad and describes many types of systems. Ask any ten managers to define the term MIS, and you will likely get ten very different answers. For a clinical manager, the information system will report on problem assessments and treatment planning. A financial manager will require a system that reports on revenues and expenses. A manager of quality assurance will require reports that compare program data against predetermined norms. These systems are all examples of an MIS because they provide the information necessary to manage. They are all different because they support the management of diverse functions.

Still, the failure to deal with the human side—not technical problems—most often causes MIS failures.

The definition of an MIS depends entirely on the function being managed. Systems that are perfectly suited to one area may be of no use in another. Simply put: one person's MIS is not for everyone.

Clarification: What an MIS is Not

Finally, don't assume that an MIS will require a computer. Besides, it is easy to underestimate the amount of support required by even the smallest of microcomputer systems. There are learning curves, back-up procedures, version numbers, release levels, and a myriad of other confusing concepts to overcome and incorporate into your operation. Using a computer can introduce a level of complexity that may completely outweigh any benefits. For this reason, use great care when making a decision to computerize. In small programs, management information can be processed manually, and this is often an excellent way to explore the benefits of an MIS before adding a computer. Computerization does *not* guarantee MIS success. Computers generate data; people define information.

PREREQUISITES FOR MIS DEVELOPMENT

Developing large-scale information systems is usually a complex task. Information requirements must be conceptualized; processing systems (hardware and software) must be designed. Still, the failure to deal with the human side—not technical problems—most often causes MIS failures. Information systems tend to impose a higher level of standardization and rationality upon organizations. They also affect jobs, career interests, management styles, and organizational politics. In short, MIS development is a risky business. Before beginning, a program director should look for three important prerequisites in the organization.

Before computerizing, a treatment director should take several preliminary steps to improve chances for success.

---

1. *Feel Need for Change.* Staff must feel the need to do something to improve information management in their organization. A desire to become "state of the art," or one staff member's enthusiasm for automation, is not sufficient reason to computerize. Staff at several levels must feel the need to make significant improvements.
2. *Have Top Management Support.* Program directors must support MIS development and implementation. Only top management can commit the necessary resources (staff time and money). MIS projects typically cross department lines, affecting areas such as rehabilitation, medical records, the business office, and support services. If the authority of

upper management is missing, any one of these departments can hinder the development of a corporate MIS.

3. *Have User Involvement.* Staff involvement is essential. Staff collect the information and receive reports. Research shows that an MIS developed without staff input can easily be ignored, or worse, sabotaged by resistant staff.

GETTING STARTED

Before computerizing, a treatment director should take several preliminary steps to improve chances for success. First, review the long-range plan for the organization. Will any new services be developed? Will the program add new locations? Will existing services be increased or decreased in volume? The answers to these types of questions will guide MIS planning.

Second, the organization's experience with management information systems should be assessed. This assessment will help to determine the overall scope of the project. If there is little experience, the project should be smaller and focus on only the most important aspects of the program. External assistance may be necessary. If there is significant experience, a larger, more encompassing project could be undertaken.

Third, think about the objectives for MIS development. Is it primarily for clinical support (patient assessment, treatment planning, clinical staff supervision, utilization review)? Should it support program management with data on patient demographics, program census, length of stay, referral sources, and method of payment? Should it also support quality assurance functions, with information on program completion rates and patient satisfaction with services? Should it include the automation of clerical and bookkeeping functions? Technically, all these functions can be computerized. In a practical sense, however, a program manager needs to clearly identify the scope of the project and keep it to a manageable size. This will require making hard choices on what to include within the project.

Finally, a program director needs to continually scan the regulatory environment to monitor the information requirements of accreditation bodies, licensors, payors, and cost-control groups. Ideally, data to meet these requirements would be built into the program's information systems. Unfortunately, these requirements change over time, making it difficult to automate external reporting. Nonetheless, anticipation will at least reduce the extent of future system modifications.

MIS Design: Working Backward

When we think of data systems, many of us think of data collection forms or computers that handle data input and processing. But we really should begin with MIS output—what we want out of the system. Once our information requirements are clear, we can define our data elements and examine our options (hardware and software) for data processing. Without clearly targeted objectives and well-defined information requirements, staff easily get lost in a maze of forms, reports, procedures, data, and computer technology.

Working backward means beginning with the management functions an MIS is intended to support. What routine program functions (such as admissions) need to be monitored? What types of data are needed for planning, marketing, budgeting, and staff supervision? How can we measure whether a program is achieving its goals? What information does the board want on a regular basis? And what will be required from oversight and review organizations? This is the place to start.

Once management needs are established, prototype reports can be drafted. Focus on the report content—the actual data that managers *need.* But do not neglect the format (the packaging) and the frequency of reports. What should reports look like? How should the data be sorted and summarized? And how often should they be run?

At this point, staff can begin defining the data needed for MIS reports. That task is not as easy as it first sounds. In a large treatment program, staff often have varying definitions for even basic terms, such as *referral sources, assessed problems,* and *discharge ratings.* These differences must be resolved so that data input can be consistent and reliable. As the data are identified, they should be organized into logical groups. For example, gender, age, and race might be part of a demographic record on each patient. These groupings will often help to identify additional data items. This is also a good time to begin thinking about the logical place and time to gather these groups of data.

Finally, data processing choices (computer hardware and software) can be considered. Here, staff are much less vulnerable to oversell. They can show a vendor—or several vendors—the types of data going into the system (input), and the types of reports coming out (output). Can the vendor put together a system that will process the input into output for a given number of records (for example, patients, transactions, or days)? How much will the system cost? How long will it take to deliver or develop it? These are the fundamental questions to ask. More specific advice on selection of computer consultants and vendors is offered later in this chapter.

MIS DEVELOPMENT: THREE OPTIONS

Three possible options for computerization are *shared time, service bureaus,* and *microcomputers.* Each has pros and cons. In *sharing time,* hospital-based programs may have access to a large central computer with tremendous capability. The problem is how much access, and when. Except for routine patient billing, hospital treatment units often receive much less attention than other hospital departments and functions.

Service bureaus can process data on a timely basis. These companies provide generic services to many users. The services offered are usually limited to common fiscal operations such as payroll and general ledger. Although these services are not usually sufficient for program management, they are typically very cost effective.

Because they are becoming increasingly affordable, powerful, and easy to use, *microcomputers* are appearing as a viable option for treatment providers. These machines can serve many functions including word processing, accounting, records and file management, mailing list storage, desktop publishing, data analysis, and graphics.

The prime consideration in evaluating different microcomputers is, of course, the range of software available to run on them. Most machines now support what is called *horizontal* market software. These are generalized packages that customers buy and use in their own way. Word processing, spreadsheet, data base, and graphics packages are typical examples of horizontal software.

There is, however, a growing market of *vertical* software for health and human services, including chemical dependency. Vertical market software is specifically designed for a particular business or industry. In the treatment field, vertical software is being developed for functions such as patient screening, assessment, treatment planning, quality assurance, and program monitoring.

MAKING CHOICES: CRITERIA FOR EVALUATING SYSTEMS

With all these hardware and software options, choosing among competing systems is difficult. The following list is a set of criteria to help make a good decision. Although several refer to a vendor—a computer equipment dealer or software consultant—these same criteria can be applied to in-house shared time systems.

1. *Suitability of Packaged Software.* A key to success is a good match between software capabilities and organizational needs. With vertical market software, the extent and cost of potential modifications should be carefully investigated. Again, defining your needs before approaching vendors will be invaluable.

2. *Vendor Support and Consultation.* Most systems require some type of ongoing technical support. Compare vendors on the support they can provide in
   - software customization
   - system installation
   - system documentation (user manuals)
   - staff training
   - technical assistance (troubleshooting)
   - product warranty (hardware and software)
   - future software upgrades

3. *Vendor as a Business Organization.* Since good customer service and support are so important, it is a good idea to become familiar with the vendor

as a business. Are the programmers at all familiar with chemical dependency treatment? If not, custom software development will be risky. Does the vendor seem to have sufficient technical expertise and experience? How long has the vendor been working with its equipment and programming languages? What is the history of the company? What is its "installed base"—the number of sites where its systems are in use? And can the vendor provide at least three customers you can contact for references?

4. *Size of the Vendor's or Consultant's Organization.* Dealing with an individual consultant can be risky. What if that person goes out of business or moves away? The computer market is still quite volatile; even a larger firm is no guarantee of longevity. Look for stability in the organization you select.

5. *Product Reliability.* Computer equipment should be reliable. The software should be free of "bugs," mistakes that corrupt the data or create improper logic or incorrect mathematical operations. These problems are commonplace in new software products.

6. *Implementation.* What will system installation entail? What will it take to convert from existing procedures and data to the new system? Will your operations be hampered during this period? Are there additional resources, such as extra staff time or rental computers, that will make this conversion smooth?

7. *Ease of Use.* Try to anticipate how difficult it will be for your staff to operate the system. How easy will it be for them to enter the data and run reports? What training is necessary and available? How and when will the training be delivered? Some studies show that proper training can cost as much as the computer system itself. A system that is "user friendly" may be much more likely to succeed.

8. *Expandability.* How many records will the system hold at a time? Can it be expanded in volume (the number of patient records, entries, or transactions)? Can you add more terminals, memory, data storage, or printers? What other types of software can be used? Generally, a system that is compatible with

other manufacturers' equipment and software is preferable.

9. *Flexibility*. Ask the vendor how difficult it will be to make changes in your data base. Also, can existing reports be modified? How difficult—and expensive—will it be to create new reports?

10. *Security of Data*. Data security is too often overlooked. Find out if computer terminals can be locked, or if passwords can be provided for users. Of course, a locked office or file cabinet can also provide a large measure of security at a low cost.

11. *Disaster Planning*. What happens if the system is stolen or damaged? Can your business continue without it? Computer problems that result in loss of data are common. Do you have a backup to reload from? What if your computer and backup are destroyed?

12. *Speed or Response Time*. Computer speed is sometimes an over-rated feature. (Usually, the person at the terminal is the slowest system component.) Still, long pauses between data entry screens or during other computer operations are frustrating and inefficient. Ask the vendor how long it will take to enter and edit a record; search and sort the data; and run and print reports.

13. *Cost Justification*. This is the most difficult series of questions to answer. Even just estimating the total costs of developing and operating a new system is not easy. Furthermore, what are the projected benefits for the organization? Finally, in view of other program needs, are the benefits worth the costs?

ASSESSMENT TOOLS: A SPECIAL CASE

If you are considering the use of a computerized patient assessment tool or diagnostic instrument, you may want to ask a few additional questions before deciding:

1. History of Tool. What is the background of this instrument? In particular, how were the original test questions developed?

2. Reliability/Validity Research. What research has been done to demonstrate that the tool is reliable (consistency over time and with different groups of patients) and valid (accurate)? Has the instrument been standardized (normed for treatment and normal populations)?

3. Output. What is the output or end result? Do you get raw scores, profiles, comparisons with treatment or normal populations, diagnoses, or diagnostic impressions? If chemical dependency is indicated, is there any recommendation for level of care?

4. Ease of Administration and Scoring. Review the instrument to assess its appropriateness, length, and reading level for your patients. (Some instruments can be taken by the patient at a terminal.) How will the test be scored? Some can be scored on-site manually or by computer. Others need to be mailed to the publisher for scoring. Also find out if the interviewer or test administrator needs any special training or credentials to use it.

5. Acceptance By Payors/Licensors. Naturally, no guarantees can be made that a particular tool or test will satisfy all accreditation bodies, licensors, and third party payors. Still, it is fair to ask what the publisher's experience has been in this area.

Using Consultants: The Vendor-Client Relationship

After evaluating your options, you may decide to hire an equipment vendor or software consultant to design and develop a customized system for you. Your contract with the consultant, however brief, is a *partnership* with mutual responsibilities, outlined below.

Vendor Responsibilities	*Client Responsibilities*
• Don't oversell	• Have realistic expectations
• Develop a clear contract	• Develop a clear contract
• Deliver on modifications	• Clearly define specifications
• Provide user training	• Conduct cross-training
• Provide system documentation	• Develop office procedures for system operation, back-up, and recovery of information
• *Listen* to client needs and problems	• Provide management support and user involvement
• Anticipate software enhancements	• Plan for future needs

Spelling out these mutual expectations—and fulfilling your own as client—will help you get the most out of your consultant or vendor.

SYSTEM IMPLEMENTATION: THE HUMAN SIDE

Care should be taken to properly implement and operate a new system. This is where a lot of failures occur, because not enough attention is paid to the behavioral side of computer systems. We should remember that it is the people who make the systems work.

New information systems can affect at least three levels of treatment staff: *clerical, clinical,* and *managerial.*

> The solution to clinical staff resistance, of course, is to involve them in the design of the computer system from the start.

Clerical staff usually enter and edit the data, run reports, and perform other "housekeeping" functions, such as file management and data backup. Understandably, clerical staff can feel threatened by changes in their existing jobs and the challenges involved in computerization. To allay these fears, provide staff training before the new system is installed. Solicit their feedback on how to best manage data entry functions. Finally, change position descriptions where necessary. Simply putting a terminal on a secretary's or clerk's desk and expecting him or her to do extensive data input, along with many other existing duties, probably will not work.

Clinical staff can also feel anxious about the impact of computerization in their area. In most programs, few data are available on counselor activity and performance. An automated patient record or quality assurance system might change that, producing data on counselors (such as case loads, units of service) and on their patients (treatment progress, program completion, satisfaction with services). Traditionally, clinical staff are unaccustomed to having these data made "public," and may resist the introduction of the new system.

The solution to clinical staff resistance, of course, is to involve them in the design of the computer system from the start. What are *their* information needs as counselors? What improvements can be made in the patient records? How can staff activity and patient progress be better defined and monitored? How can MIS data be used to improve treatment effectiveness? If staff are involved from the beginning, they will be much more supportive when a system is installed.

The information resource, like human and fiscal resources, needs to be managed.

Finally, a new MIS will obviously affect the program *managers* it is designed to support. More formalized information systems have an impact on managerial styles. In the past, managers have relied on a more *traditional* style of supervision, characterized by face-to-face communications, informal relationships, and intuitive decision making. Improved management information promotes a more rational style, however, based on written communications, formal information channels, and informed decision-making. As with clinical staff, more data are made public on program functioning and staff performance. In this environment, leadership styles based on personal influence are less effective than ones based on information.

Again, the solution to any resistance is to involve managers in the design and development of the system from the start. If the system really is decision-centered—rather than data-centered—its usefulness to program administrators should be apparent. Timing reports to coincide with management cycles (such as annual budgets, accreditation site visits, board reports) will also increase utilization.

MANAGING INFORMATION AS A RESOURCE

The information resource, like human and fiscal resources, needs to be managed. Program administrators need to manage the development, installation, and operation of information systems in their organizations. Thinking about your program's information needs, getting involved in the design of your systems, and supporting the new system will increase your chances of success with computerization.

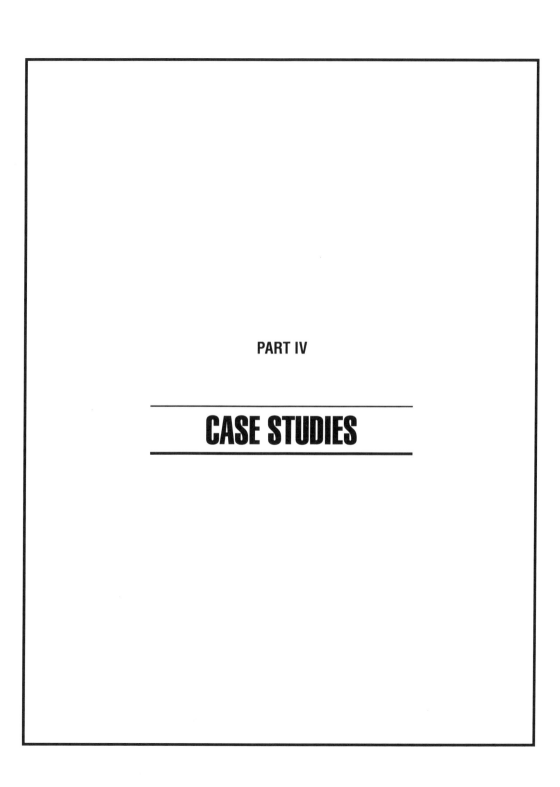

PART IV

CASE STUDIES

CHAPTER NINE

TREATMENT OUTCOMES FOR MINNESOTA MODEL PROGRAMS

Paul Higgins, Ph.D.; Ruth Baeumler;
Jeanne Fisher; and Victoria Johnson*

*These authors are members of the Research
Consultation Department of Hazelden Services,
Inc. In this chapter, they summarize data from
several treatment centers, including Hazelden.*

OVERVIEW

In this chapter, we present patient profile and outcome data from a sample of seven adult residential and inpatient programs representing part of the Hazelden Evaluation Consortium. These programs also represent three of the four U.S. Census regions (West, North Central, and South). Each program embodies the Minnesota Model approach to treatment and recovery.

Our purpose here is to explore the relationships among patient characteristics, program characteristics, and treatment outcomes for these programs—with particular focus on factors that may be responsible for variations in rates of post-treatment alcohol and illicit-drug abstinence. Data from the Hazelden Primary Rehabilitation Program in Center City, Minnesota, are also presented for additional benchmark comparisons. Each of these seven programs—

* We acknowledge the data processing contributions of Barb Dowell and the staff of Hazelden's Information Services Department.

and the Hazelden program—employ the same methodology for patient follow-up and program evaluation.

A major strength of a standardized consortium approach to evaluation is that it allows use of either treatment programs or patients as a unit of analysis. We emphasize analysis based on treatment programs: for example, patient, treatment, and outcome profiles are constructed by using treatment program averages, with each program regarded as an equivalent case and given equal weight. The research design does, however, include a random sample of patients from the consortium treatment programs to enable supplementary correlational analysis.

THE HAZELDEN EVALUATION CONSORTIUM

The Hazelden Evaluation Consortium includes treatment centers that have contracted with the Research Consultation Department of Hazelden Services, Inc., in Minneapolis, for the conduct of some or all of their patient follow-up and program evaluation activities.

The Hazelden Primary Rehabilitation Program in Center City, part of the Evaluation Consortium, originated the basic mail-and-telephone-survey program-evaluation approach used by the consortium. The evaluation of Hazelden's own program, however, is conducted by Hazelden's Planning and Evaluation Department, also in Center City. This department is separate from the Research Consultation Department that conducts evaluations for other consortium members. Another report focuses on Hazelden's patient characteristics and treatment outcomes for those discharged during 1978-1983 (Gilmore et al. 1986).

To ease comparative analysis, the Evaluation Consortium and the Hazelden Primary Rehabilitation Program are discussed as separate entities, although the Hazelden Primary Rehabilitation Program is part of the consortium.

The total group of fourteen consortium members having residential or inpatient chemical dependency programs that were evaluated by Hazelden during 1986-1988 are listed on pages 112 and 113. An icon (❖) indicates client programs that collected their own survey data, in consultation with Hazelden. Hazelden then prepared evaluation reports based on these data.

Note that data in this chapter are based on surveys of patients admitted to seven of the fourteen member programs of the consortium, primarily during 1986 and 1987. Programs were selected because they each had response rates of 50 percent or more for patient follow-up surveys conducted at six and twelve months post-treatment.

METHODOLOGICAL CONCERNS ABOUT FOLLOW-UP EVALUATION OF CHEMICAL DEPENDENCY PROGRAMS

In this chapter, we do not extensively respond to current criticisms of outcome evaluation of chemical dependency programs (Longabaugh and Lewis 1988). A principal criticism concerns the reliability and validity of patient self-reports about post-treatment use of alcohol and illicit drugs. Some researchers, Fuller (1988), for example, feel that abstinence rates based on self-reports are generally underestimates, where others may be concerned about overestimates.

Research by Krueger, conducted in 1985, however, supports the reliability of Hazelden follow-up data. What follows are examples that list good-faith efforts by Hazelden departments and the Evaluation Consortium to obtain reliable follow-up data:

- Questionnaires and survey methods have been revised for greater clarity. Internal consistency studies (Krueger) suggest that survey items have acceptable reliability.
- Corresponding information is obtained separately from both patients and confirming sources (for example, significant others or "S.O.s"). Because twelve-month questionnaires for the former patient and the significant other have the same questions about (1) former patient's alcohol use, (2) former patient's other drug use, and (3) former patient's AA/NA attendance, comparisons of patient versus S.O. responses can be used to check the validity of the patient's reported adjustment data. In both Krueger's research and in more consortium evaluation studies, these comparisons show
  - Similar responses from patients versus S.O.s on these questions, particularly on alcohol use.

- ■ A high percentage of agreement (usually 60-80 percent) between matched patient and S.O. pairs in their exact responses to each of the three questions.
- ■ Overall, patients usually report slightly higher levels of abstinence from alcohol and illicit drugs, and more frequent AA attendance, than do confirming sources; however, consortium experience suggests that Fuller overstates the inaccuracy of this methodological problem. Consortium results generally support the validity of patient self-reports for evaluation of program effectiveness.

- The policy of consortium programs is to include in follow-up research any former patient likely to answer a mail or telephone survey. In practice, all programs have excluded some patients because they were inappropriate or unavailable for follow-up (for example, stayed less than five days in treatment, refused to grant survey permission, returned to treatment, were incarcerated, or died).
- In conducting follow-up research for large programs, it is not cost effective or statistically necessary to survey the entire treatment population. In such cases, careful random sampling is used, and high response rates are sought—to increase the likelihood that data collected are representative of the program population. Generally, a response rate of 65 percent is a desirable benchmark, while 50 percent is an acceptable minimum. We avoid doing anything that could alter response rates: sheer inability to reach a patient by phone or mail, despite repeated attempts, is not grounds for excluding him or her from response rate calculations.
- Consortium program evaluations include a comparison of survey respondents and nonrespondents with respect to several important demographic and treatment characteristics. Such a comparison can support outcome results from respondents as being representative of the total treatment population. Experience suggests that if response rates meet or exceed the benchmark (65 percent), there is considerable overlap between

the distributions of respondents versus nonrespondents with respect to key characteristics.
When response rates are relatively low (below 50
percent), however, those responding are more
likely to be female, to be older, and to have completed treatment with staff approval.

While they are aware of recent methodological critiques
of chemical dependency research, those composing the
Hazelden Evaluation Consortium use methods and procedures that obviate much of the criticism that has been lev-
eled against chemical dependency program evaluation.
Evidence from consortium studies supports the validity
and usefulness of patient self-reports for evaluation of program effectiveness. For most consortium program evaluations, the observed abstinence rates, AA/NA attendance,
and other profile and outcome statistics probably approxi-
mate the true state of affairs in the entire post-treatment
population of patients who have had at least a minimal
(greater than five days) exposure to treatment.

ELEMENTS OF THE HAZELDEN EVALUATION SYSTEM

The Hazelden evaluation system, used by consortium
members, consists of the following three components:

1. *A clinical record abstract component,* the source of
   data for the Patient Profile and Treatment Profile
   sections of this chapter.
2. *A patient satisfaction-assessment component,* based
   on Service Evaluation Questionnaires (see
   Appendix B) completed by patients at discharge.
   These questionnaires provide detailed feedback to
   programs about patients' reactions to various
   aspects of treatment.
3. *A post-treatment follow-up component,* which we
   discuss later in this chapter. Questionnaires are
   mailed to former patients at six and twelve
   months following discharge—with telephone interviewing of nonrespondents to increase the
   response rate. In addition, twelve months after
   treatment, questionnaires and telephone inter-

views are conducted with each patient's significant other. Designated at the time of discharge by the patient, the S.O. is a person close to the patient, who is aware of the patient's post-treatment progress. As discussed previously, patient versus significant other responses to the same questions can be compared to check the validity of patients' self-reported adjustment.

During the 1985-1987 period studied, about half of the treatment programs in the consortium asked Hazelden Research Consultation Department to conduct all mail and telephone surveying of former patients. The remaining members of the consortium conducted their own survey activity using Hazelden forms, with the completed forms mailed to Hazelden for analysis and reporting.

The Sample of Consortium Programs

Seven of the fourteen consortium programs were selected for study. Again, programs were selected because they each had response rates of 50 percent or more for patient follow-up surveys conducted at six and twelve months post-treatment. These programs represented 3,116 admissions.

All data in this chapter are based on patients *admitted* during either 1986 or a period (depending on the program's Hazelden contract) that included portions of both 1986 and 1987—with two exceptions:

- Surveys for one of the programs covered patients admitted July 1985 through June 1986.
- Hazelden six-month data are from a survey of patients *discharged* during 1986; twelve-month data are based on 1985 discharges.

The Sample of Consortium Patients

To supplement the analysis based on treatment programs, a patient-based analysis was conducted, using a random sample of two hundred patients drawn from the five consortium programs (forty from each) that had the highest response rates. These five programs were also geographically and demographically representative of the

Evaluation Consortium, and are likely representative of treatment programs that, like Hazelden's, are based on the Twelve Steps.

We again emphasize that this analysis is based on treatment centers as units of analysis; for example, patient, treatment, and outcome profiles are constructed by combining treatment program averages—with each program regarded as independent and given equal weight. To supplement these treatment program data, however, an analysis using patients as the units of analysis was also conducted.

We report information concerning only a sample of the key variables studied during a typical consortium program evaluation.

PATIENT PROFILE

The following patient profile (table 9.1) is based on analysis of treatment center aggregate data.

Because of random sampling or exclusion from follow-up, for each program the N in the initial follow-up sample is less than the total N of patients admitted during the period studied. Hence, Patient Profile results are based on all 3,116 admissions to the seven consortium programs, plus 1,655 Hazelden Primary Rehabilitation Program admissions. The six-month survey results are based on 1,286 consortium admissions and 1,077 Hazelden admissions; and the twelve-month survey results are based on 1,154 consortium admissions and 352 Hazelden admissions. The large difference in Ns between Hazelden's six- and twelve-month survey results is largely due to a change in the procedure used for random sampling.

For each patient characteristic, seven individual program averages have been combined into a single consortium average and compared with the average from the Hazelden Primary Rehabilitation Program. The range of program averages within the consortium is also shown.

- *Gender.* Among consortium programs and Hazelden, about 70 percent of the patients were male.
- *Age.* The median age was thirty-two for the consortium and between thirty-five and thirty-six for Hazelden patients.

Does Your Program Measure Up?

TABLE 9.1
PATIENT PROFILE

Demographic	7 treatment programs (N=3,116)			Hazelden* (N=1,655)
	Low	Mean	High	
Gender				
Male	57%	71%	84%	70%
Female	16%	29%	43%	30%
Age				
17 and younger	0%	4%	14%	0%#
18-29	24%	34%	43%	25%#
30-39	21%	32%	49%	35%#
40-49	10%	15%	20%	20%#
50-59	4%	10%	17%	15%#
60-69	0%	4%	7%	5%#
70 and older	<1%	1%	2%	1%#
Median age in years	29	32@	38	35-36#
Marital Status				
Married	33%	39%	47%	44%
Single	22%	30%	46%	33%
Divorced or separated	16%	23%	37%	20%
Other	2%	5%	14%	2%
No answer	0%	3%	17%	<1%
Education				
No High School diploma	4%	22%	36%	5%
High School diploma or General Equivalency Diploma	10%	33%	38%	26%
Some post-secondary	23%	28%	35%	27%
College or advanced degree	1%	14%	38%	41%
No answer	0%	3%	5%	<1%

Note: In this and all subsequent tables, the means are based on an equal weighing of all 7 programs. Percentages may not total 100 percent due to rounding error.
* 1986 data.
# Estimated from a distribution with different age categories.
@ Median of program medians.

- *Marital status.* An estimated 39 percent of consortium patients and 44 percent of Hazelden patients were married.
- *Education.* An estimated 42 percent of consortium patients had at least some post-secondary education, including 14 percent with college or advanced degrees. The corresponding figures for the Hazelden patients were 68 percent and 41 percent, respectively. One of the consortium programs, however, equaled Hazelden in average educational level.

Patients Report After Six Months: Their Chemical Dependency Problem When Admitted to Treatment

Based on their recall six months after treatment, the most frequent chemical dependency problem for consortium patients at admission was alcohol use only (for about one-half of the patients). This was followed by those who reported combined use of alcohol and other drugs (about one-third). Table 9.2 illustrates this. There was some variation among individual programs in these statistics, however. A minority—never more than 29 percent for a single

TABLE 9.2

CHEMICAL DEPENDENCY PROBLEM AT TIME OF ADMISSION

(BASED ON PATIENT SURVEY AT SIX MONTHS POST-TREATMENT)

Problem	7 treatment programs (N=1,286)			Hazelden* (N=1,077)
	Low	Mean	High	
Alcohol only	33%	46%	58%	45%
Other mood-altering drugs	9%	17%	29%	1%
Both alcohol and other mood-altering drugs	26%	32%	40%	54%
Neither alcohol nor other drugs	1%	3%	8%	0%
No answer	0%	1%	3%	0%

* Reference for these statistics (based on 1983 admissions) is a *Hazelden Brief Report.* (See References on page 114.)

program—was admitted for sole use of drugs other than alcohol. Corresponding figures for Hazelden (based on 1983 data) show that nearly one-half were admitted for alcohol use only; 54 percent for combined use of alcohol and other drugs; but only 1 percent reported sole use of drugs other than alcohol.

TREATMENT PROFILE

On the average, as shown in table 9.3, both the consortium patients and the Hazelden patients had the same

- *length of stay* (a median 28 days)
- *proportion discharged with staff approval* (80-85 percent)

Clients' Overall Satisfaction with Treatment Services

Respondents were asked, at both six and twelve months after treatment, to rate their overall satisfaction with the services they had received.

- At six months after treatment, an average 68 percent of consortium respondents said they were "very satisfied" with the services they had received, while 25 percent were "mostly satisfied" (corresponding detail unavailable for Hazelden).
- At twelve months after treatment, 71 percent of consortium respondents indicated they were "very satisfied," with 19 percent "mostly satisfied."

When the two ratings "very" and "mostly" satisfied were combined, overall satisfaction was high at both survey points and was similar for both the consortium programs and Hazelden (90-97 percent).

PATIENT OUTCOMES AT SIX AND
TWELVE MONTHS AFTER TREATMENT

Response rates for both the six- and twelve-month surveys were higher, on the average, for Hazelden than for

TABLE 9.3
TREATMENT PROFILE

Item	7 treatment programs			Hazelden*
	Low	Mean	High	
		(N=3,116)		(N=1,655)
Length of stay#				
Median	21 days	28 days @	35 days	28 days*
Discharged with staff approval				
Yes	80%	85%	90%	81%*
No	10%	<15%	20%	19%
No answer	0%	<1%	1%	0%*
Overall satisfaction with treatment services rated at –				
6 months after treatment		(N=1,286)		(N=1,077)
Very or mostly satisfied	88%	93%	98%	93%
Very satisfied	54%	68%	81%	–
Mostly satisfied	17%	25%	35%	–
Indifferent or dissatisfied	1%	5%	10%	3%
No answer	1%	2%	4%	4%
12 months after treatment		(N=1,154)		(N=308)
Very or mostly satisfied	83%	90%	97%	97%
Very satisfied	61%	71%	87%	81%
Mostly satisfied	10%	19%	32%	16%
Indifferent or dissatisfied	2%	7%	17%	0%
No answer	0%	3%	5%	3%

Note: Blanks indicate data not available. Overall satisfaction ratings based on survey data.
* 1986 data.
# Ns on which this statistic is based may be slightly(but not more than 1%) less than the program Ns in the column headings.
@ Median of program medians.

the consortium, although two individual programs approximated the Hazelden response rates (table 9.4).

- *Six-month response rates:* the consortium's overall response rate, based on an initial sample of 2,074 patients, was 62 percent. For Hazelden, the corresponding rate was 76 percent. Three consor-

Does Your Program Measure Up?

Table 9.4
Follow-Up Survey Response Rates

Item		Program with –		7-program total	Hazelden
		Lowest rate	Highest rate		
6-month survey					
Initial sample of patients	N=	537	394	2,074	1,417
Patients responding	N=	295	306	1,286	1,077
Response rate	%=	55%	78%	**62%**	**76%**
12-month survey					
Initial sample of patients	N=	115	388	2,066	352
Patients responding	N=	38	296	1,154	252
Response rate	%=	33%	76%	**56%**	**72%**

tium programs, plus Hazelden, exceeded the benchmark of 65 percent, while none fell below the minimum target of 50 percent.

- *Twelve-month response rates:* the consortium achieved 56 percent, based on a sample of 2,066 patients; the Hazelden rate was 72 percent. Hazelden and two consortium programs exceeded the benchmark, and one (at 33 percent) fell below the minimum target.

Alcohol and Illicit Drug Use
At Six and Twelve Months After Treatment

How were these patients faring with respect to alcohol and illicit drug use at six and twelve months after discharge? Table 9.5 shows that at six months after treatment, consortium respondents and Hazelden respondents were roughly equivalent in their rates of alcohol use, illicit drug use, and combined abstinence from alcohol and illicit drugs.

TABLE **9.5**

ALCOHOL AND ILLICIT DRUG USE AT **6** MONTHS POST-TREATMENT

Item	7 treatment programs (N=1,286)			Hazelden* (N=1,077)
	Low	Mean	High	
	Compared to use before treatment –			
Alcohol use				
Not used	50%	64%	73%	66%
Not as much	NA	29%	NA	30%
About as much	NA	6%	NA	3%
Use more	NA	2%	NA	<1%
No answer	0%	1%	2%	1%
Illicit drug use				
Not used*	67%	77%	82%	84%
Not as much	NA	11%	NA	10%
About as much	NA	3%	NA	<1%
Use more	NA	3%	NA	<1%
No answer	2%	6%	9%	5%
Combined abstinence from alcohol and illicit drugs				
Abstinent*	43%	57%	65%	61%
Not abstinent	NA	36%	NA	34%
No answer	2%	7%	11%	5%

* Use of drugs for medical reasons does not affect abstinence status.
NA=Not Available

At twelve months after treatment, as illustrated in table 9.6, Hazelden patients appeared to have higher abstinence rates than consortium patients for both alcohol and illicit drugs.

At each interval after treatment, and for both alcohol and drugs, however, several individual consortium programs approximated or exceeded Hazelden's abstinence rates. Specifically:

- *Alcohol Use*
  - When surveyed six months after discharge, an estimated 64 percent of consortium patients

Does Your Program Measure Up?

TABLE **9.6**

ALCOHOL AND ILLICIT DRUG USE AT **12** MONTHS POST-TREATMENT

Item	7 treatment programs (N=1,154)			Hazelden* (N=308)
	Low	Mean	High	
	Compared to use before treatment –			
Alcohol use				
Not used	37%	54%	66%	66%
Not as much	NA	35%	NA	
About as much	NA	6%	NA	
Use more	NA	2%	NA	
No answer	0%	3%	10%	3%
Illicit drug use				
Not used*	60%	70%	81%	78%
Not as much	NA	14%	NA	
About as much	NA	5%	NA	
Use more	NA	2%	NA	
No answer	3%	10%	18%	11%
Combined abstinence from alcohol and illicit drugs				
Abstinent*	30%	46%	59%	~60% (estimate)
Not abstinent	NA	43%	NA	
No answer	2%	11%	28%	

NA= Not Available

* Use of drugs for medical reasons does not affect abstinence status.

and 66 percent of Hazelden patients indicated they had not used alcohol since treatment.

■ At twelve months, the Hazelden sobriety rate remained stable at 66 percent, whereas the consortium average had dropped to 54 percent.

- *Illicit Drug Use*
  - At six months, an estimated 77 percent of consortium patients and 84 percent of Hazelden patients claimed post-treatment abstinence* from drugs other than alcohol.
  - At twelve months, both the consortium and the Hazelden abstinence rates had dropped to 70 percent and 78 percent, respectively.
- *Combined Abstinence*
  - When surveyed six months post-treatment, an estimated 57 percent of consortium respondents and 61 percent of Hazelden respondents indicated abstinence from both alcohol and illicit drugs.
  - Hazelden patients, at twelve months post-treatment, apparently had an advantage over the consortium patients with respect to combined abstinence, with estimated rates of 60 percent versus 46 percent, respectively. Again, the Hazelden rate, unlike the consortium average, appeared to change little. Two consortium programs, however, were able to sustain combined abstinence rates of about 60 percent at six months after treatment.
- *The Range in Abstinence Among Consortium Programs*
  - The range was particularly high for alcohol abstinence and combined abstinence. At six months after treatment, alcohol abstinence ranged from 50 to 73 percent, while combined abstinence ranged from 43 percent to 65 percent. At twelve months after treatment, the gap between the highest and lowest rates for these two variables had widened. Alcohol abstinence then ranged from 37 percent to 66 percent, while combined abstinence ranged from 30 percent to 59 percent. The graphics of figure 9.1 compare the average six-month rate of abstinence of the consortium to its average twelve-month rate.

---

* Included within the drug-abstinent groups were all respondents who had used a prescription drug or drug of that nature for medical reasons only.

Does Your Program Measure Up?

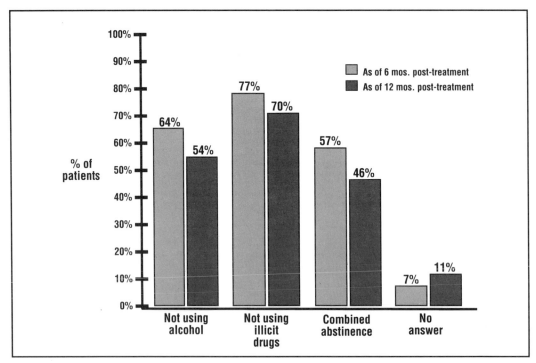

FIGURE 9.1

THE CONSORTIUM'S AVERAGE ALCOHOL AND OTHER DRUG ABSTINENCE RATES
AT 6 VS. 12 MONTHS POST-TREATMENT
(N=7 PROGRAMS)

AA and NA Attendance:
Six Versus Twelve Months After Treatment

In general, AA/NA attendance among the consortium programs was lower than that of Hazelden, and decreased from six to twelve months after treatment; whereas Hazelden's higher AA/NA attendance rate was apparently quite stable over a one-year period (see figure 9.2 and table 9.7).

- At six months after treatment, the average weekly AA/NA attendance rate among consortium patients was 51 percent; the corresponding Hazelden estimate was 64 percent. Overall AA/NA participation (including respondents who attended

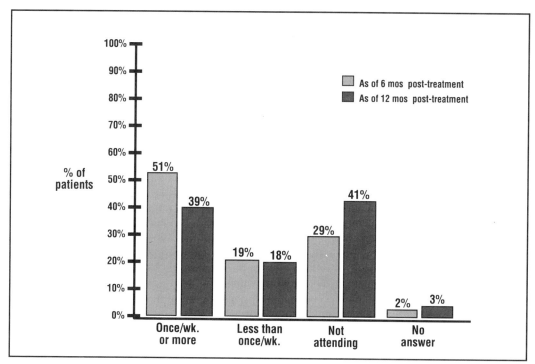

FIGURE 9.2
THE CONSORTIUM'S AVERAGE AA/NA ATTENDANCE
AT 6 VS. 12 MONTHS POST-TREATMENT
(N=7 PROGRAMS)

less than once a week) was 70 percent for the consortium and 78 percent for Hazelden.

- At twelve months after treatment, Hazelden weekly attendance had apparently changed little; however, the average consortium weekly rate had dropped to 39 percent, along with a drop in overall participation to 57 percent.

- Again, individual consortium programs (two) outperformed the consortium as a whole by sustaining AA/NA attendance rates similar to those of Hazelden (about 70-80 percent) over the six- to twelve-month post-treatment interval.

TABLE 9.7
ATTENDANCE AT AA/NA MEETINGS AT 6 VS. 12 MONTHS POST-TREATMENT

Item	7 treatment programs			Hazelden
	Low	Mean	High	
6 months post-treatment		(N=1,286)		(N=1,077)
Once a week or more	36%	51%	63%	64%
Less than once a week	NA	19%	NA	14%
Not attending	NA	29%	NA	20%
No answer	<1%	2%	4%	2%
12 months post-treatment		(N=1,154)		(N=308)
Once a week or more	22%	39%	58%	62%
Less than once a week	NA	18%	NA	15%
Not attending	NA	41%	NA	22%
No answer	0%	3%	12%	1%

Note: For some programs, patients were only surveyed concerning AA attendance; therefore, some percentages in this table may slightly underestimate total AA/NA attendance.
NA= Not Available

Assessment of Life Quality Following Treatment

In addition to sobriety, abstinence from other drugs, and participation in an aftercare program that includes AA/NA, all programs studied sought improvement in patients' overall quality of life. The six- and twelve-month surveys each asked respondents for a somewhat different global assessment of life quality.

- The six-month survey asked patients to rate change in "overall quality of life" since the period before treatment. An average 82 percent of consortium patients and 90 percent of Hazelden patients gave ratings of "much" or "somewhat" improved (see table 9.8).
- The twelve-month survey asked patients to rate change in "general enjoyment of life." Similarly, an average 79 percent of consortium patients and 88 percent of Hazelden patients gave ratings of "much" or "somewhat" improved (table 9.9).

TABLE 9.8
CHANGE IN OVERALL QUALITY OF LIFE
FROM PRE-TREATMENT TO 6 MONTHS POST-TREATMENT

Rating	7 treatment programs (N=1,090)			Hazelden (N=1,077)
	Low	Mean	High	
Much or somewhat improved	70%	82%	91%	90%
Same, worse	NA	15%	NA	9%
No answer	2%	3%	6%	1%

NA= Not Available

TABLE 9.9
CHANGE IN GENERAL ENJOYMENT OF LIFE
FROM PRE-TREATMENT TO 12 MONTHS POST-TREATMENT

Rating	5 treatment programs* (N=597)			Hazelden (N=308)
	Low	Mean	High	
Much or somewhat improved	73%	79%	84%	88%
Same, worse	NA	18%	NA	NA
No answer	3%	3%	3%	NA

* Patients of 2 programs were not asked this question.
NA= Not Available

- In short, on two different quality of life measures, substantial majorities of about 80-90 percent of respondents saw general improvement at both six and twelve months after treatment. Again, though the Hazelden ratings were somewhat higher than the consortium averages, the ratings of several individual consortium programs approximated those of Hazelden.

THE STRENGTH OF A CONSORTIUM EVALUATION

We have illustrated the various information that chemical dependency treatment programs can garner from program evaluation, particularly when such evaluation is conducted in association with other treatment programs. It may also be apparent that program evaluation often leads to new insights and questions. A major strength of a standardized consortium approach to evaluation is that either treatment programs or patients can be used as the unit of analysis.

- The consortium approach to evaluation allows a member program to monitor its patient characteristics, treatment characteristics, and patient outcomes over time and in relation to other programs. Such comparative analysis can be used to establish program goals or benchmarks.
- These data can also be used to explore relationships among these variables to increase our knowledge concerning what constitutes effective treatment. The Hazelden Evaluation Consortium encourages members to share information and hypotheses concerning which program changes may have led to greater or lesser improvements in program effectiveness. Such an information exchange is conducted formally each year when member programs convene at Hazelden for a consortium conference.

We hope that at this point the practical value and cost effectiveness of conducting follow-up evaluations of chemical dependency programs are apparent. It may also be apparent from the analyses conducted here that program evaluation often leads to new insights and new questions.

CONSORTIUM PROGRAM MEMBERS

We thank these programs, members of the Hazelden Evaluation Consortium, for their support:

- Aurora Chemical Dependency Program of Reid Memorial Hospital; Richmond, Indiana❖

- Bedford Medical Center Chemical Dependency Unit; Bedford, Indiana
- Betty Ford Center at Eisenhower Medical Center; Rancho Mirage, California
- Charlotte Treatment Center (recently renamed Amethyst); Charlotte, North Carolina*
- The Edgewood Program of the Chemical Dependency Department; St. John's Mercy Medical Center, St. Louis, Missouri*
- Federal Medical Center Chemical Dependency Unit; Rochester, Minnesota
- Henry Ford Medical Center Chemical Dependency Programs (two residential programs: Maplegrove Center and Detroit Center); West Bloomfield, Michigan
- Kettle Moraine Hospital; Oconomowoc, Wisconsin*
- People Serving People, McKenna Residence; Minneapolis, Minnesota
- Rapides Chemical Dependency Services, Rapides Regional Medical Center; Alexandria, Louisiana*
- St. Catherine's Benet Lake Center, St. Catherine's Hospital; Benet Lake, Wisconsin*
- Sunrise Center, Palomar Pomerado Hospital; Poway, California
- Tau Center, Our Lady of the Lakes Regional Medical Center; Baton Rouge, Louisiana*
- Wheaton Franciscan Services, Inc.—Milwaukee, Alcohol and Drug Treatment Centers, Elmbrook Memorial Hospital; Brookfield, Wisconsin*

---

* Denotes client programs that collected their own survey data.

REFERENCES

Fuller, Richard K. "Can treatment outcome research rely on alcoholics' self-reports?" *Alcohol Health and Research World* 12 (1988): 181-86.

Gilmore, Kathleen, Donald Jones, and Leslie Tamble. "Treatment benchmarks." Photoduplicated report, 1986. (Available from Research Consultation Department, Hazelden Services, Inc., 1400 Park Avenue South, Minneapolis, MN 55404.)

Krueger, Richard A. "Validity and reliability of Hazelden treatment follow-up data." Photoduplicated report, 1985. (Available from Planning and Evaluation Department, Hazelden Foundation, Box 11, Center City, MN 55012.)

Laundergan, J.C. *Easy Does It! Alcoholism Treatment Outcomes, Hazelden and the Minnesota Model.* Center City, Minn.: Hazelden Educational Materials, 1982,

Longabaugh, Richard, and David C. Lewis. "Key issues in treatment outcome studies." *Alcohol Health and Research World* 12 (1986): 168-75.

Planning and Evaluation Department, Hazelden Foundation. "Hazelden brief report: The question of treatment effectiveness." Photoduplicated report, undated. (Available from Planning and Evaluation Department, Hazelden Foundation, Box 11, Center City, MN 55012.)

CHAPTER TEN

THE CHEMICAL ABUSE TREATMENT OUTCOME REGISTRY (CATOR):

TREATMENT OUTCOME FOR PRIVATE PROGRAMS

Norman G. Hoffmann, Ph.D., and
Patricia Ann Harrison, M.A.

Norman Hoffmann and Patricia Ann Harrison are associates with CATOR, an organization providing consultation services, and are well-known researchers in the field of chemical dependency.

A BACKGROUND

Throughout the 1970s, people increasingly questioned the efficacy of chemical dependency treatment. Critics of treatment unloaded gloomy statistics based on studies of skid-row alcoholics and pronounced that treatment had little, if any, impact on the course of alcoholism or other drug addiction. Since large-scale systematic studies of patients treated at private treatment centers had not been conducted, we had a void of empirical evidence to support treatment success.

Although treatment program administrators and staff had only testimonials to attest to the benefit of treatment, they had plenty of those. They understood the challenge, however: how to document the effectiveness of treatment without bursting the seams of tight treatment budgets.

Treatment program directors in the Minneapolis-St. Paul metropolitan area began a feasible plan to collaborate on treatment outcome evaluation. They agreed to use a standardized set of forms and procedures to collect information on patients in treatment and for follow-up contacts. Project costs would be minimized because the committee would design data collection instruments; treatment center staff would collect patient data during treatment and conduct follow-up telephone interviews. Primary expenses would be from data processing and data analysis.

Participants were well aware of the limitations and drawbacks of the project design and knew that the patient registry did not approach requisites for experimental research. Yet, with so little known about what happened to patients after treatment, compromises in research design, necessitated by budget restrictions were deemed acceptable provided that study limitations were recognized and disseminated responsibly along with the results.

With the signing of the joint agreement, the Chemical Abuse Treatment Outcome Registry (CATOR) was born. CATOR was initiated in 1979 under the auspices of the Ramsey Foundation to serve the seven treatment programs that participated in the registry design. The project was to collect data on patients in treatment for one year, with two years of follow-up. As time went by, other treatment programs, both within and outside of Minnesota, wanted to join the registry. CATOR became a service of the Ramsey Clinic Department of Psychiatry in St. Paul. Improvements were made. Chief among these was centralizing follow-up telephone interviews from the CATOR offices, rather than from participating treatment centers. Follow-up methods were improved and more tightly controlled, and patient contact rates improved.

The outcome results described in this chapter are based on two cohorts of adult inpatients (or their significant others) in the CATOR registry. The first is a group from five Minneapolis-St. Paul area programs, comprised of 1,001 patients who entered treatment between January 1983 and March 1984. The second is a group from twenty-two programs in twelve states that includes 2,303 patients who entered treatment between April 1984 and March 1986. Both groups of patients (or their significant others) were interviewed four times after discharge—at six, twelve, eighteen, and twenty-four months. Obviously, outcome of patients who are successfully contacted for consecutive follow-up interviews may differ from those who cannot be reached or who refuse to participate. Thus, patients who are successfully followed do not represent all patients who have gone through treatment. This important issue of sample bias will be addressed later in the chapter.

SAMPLE DESCRIPTION

Group One, as discussed in this chapter, includes the first cohort of patients (those in treatment in 1983 and the first quarter of 1984). Group Two consists of patients in treatment during the last three quarters of 1984, all of 1985, and the first quarter of 1986. Group One, though all treated at Minnesota centers, includes many patients (23 percent) from other parts of the United States. Group Two, while comprised of patient populations from twenty-two programs in twelve states is also predominantly a Midwest-based sample (70 percent). Primarily because of the geographic locations of the treatment centers, as well as the fact that the patients entered treatment in the early to middle 1980s, illicit drug use other than marijuana is slight. These groups do not reflect the startling increase in cocaine use seen in urban centers on the East and West Coasts at the time or in the Midwest more recently.

Table 10.1 provides a comparison of the sociodemographic profiles of the two groups. Both are predominantly male and almost exclusively white. The majority of the patients in both groups are married, and more than 80 percent in each group have at least a high school education. The second group is considerably younger: only about 20 percent are age fifty or over in Group Two compared with 28 percent in Group One.

Group Two also includes a higher proportion of patients employed full-time, likely created by the higher proportion of men in this group and their younger average age (fewer are retired). The treatment admission described in this study is the first admission for two-thirds of both groups. Of the patients who had entered treatment before, two-thirds had only one previous admission.

Although detailed socioeconomic information is unavailable on both groups, the samples can be described as pre-

TABLE 10.1
SOCIODEMOGRAPHICS OF TWO CATOR GROUPS

	Group 1 N=1,001	Group 2 N=2,303		Group 1 N=1,001	Group 2 N=2,303
SEX					
Male	67.8%	74.1%	50-59	15.0%	12.3%
Female	32.2%	25.9%	60-69	9.1%	5.8%
			70 and over	4.2%	1.7%
ETHNICITY					
White	98.4%	93.9%	**EDUCATION**		
Black	1.0%	4.4%	No degree	17.4%	17.9%
Hispanic	0.3%	0.7%	High school diploma	66.5%	69.9%
Native American	0.3%	0.9%	College degree	10.5%	8.5%
Asian and Other	0.0%	0.1%	Graduate degree	5.6%	3.8%
MARITIAL STATUS			**EMPLOYMENT**		
Married	54.9%	55.6%	Full-time employment	56.1%	65.4%
Never married	26.1%	21.3%	Part-time employment	6.1%	5.3%
Divorced	9.5%	12.4%	Unemployed	15.3%	13.8%
Separated	4.7%	4.9%	Retired/disabled	11.3%	7.5%
Widowed	4.5%	2.7%	Homemaker	6.8%	4.7%
Living with mate	0.3%	3.1%	Student	4.4%	3.3%
AGE			**PREVIOUS CHEMICAL DEPENDENCY TREATMENT**		
Under 20	5.8%	4.3%	None	68.0%	71.8%
20-29	22.5%	27.4%	One time	22.1%	19.2%
30-39	26.6%	30.0%	Two times	5.6%	4.8%
40-49	16.8%	18.5%	Three or more times	4.3%	4.2%

Note: Percentages in this and subsequent tables may not total 100 percent, due to rounding error.

dominantly middle class. Most patients had at least part of their treatment costs covered by a health insurance plan.

The aggregate profile for *all* patients who entered treatment at the participating centers during the study periods differs in significant respects. The *total* population included more minority patients (11 percent), primarily Blacks, more patients who were unmarried (57 percent) or unemployed (22 percent), more who had dropped out of high school (24 percent), and more who had previous chemical dependency treatment (36 percent). In addition, the total population included many more drug users and multiple substance users than the groups in the follow-up samples. Obviously, all these factors, which are more common in the total population than in the follow-up samples, are associated with a poorer prognosis (except for racial minority status). Thus, the favorable bias of the follow-up samples will have to be considered in the interpretation of outcome statistics.

Alcohol and Other Drug Abuse

As illustrated in table 10.2, alcohol was by far the predominant substance of abuse of the two studied groups. Roughly half were daily drinkers during the year before treatment.

One in five used marijuana at least once a week. With the exception of marijuana and alcohol, no drug was used weekly by as many as 10 percent of the patients. Although regular use of drugs other than alcohol and marijuana was uncommon, many patients did use other drugs: roughly one in five used cocaine during the year before treatment; the same proportion used amphetamines or other stimulants and tranquilizers. Approximately one patient in ten used sedatives or tranquilizers, the same prevalence of use seen for hallucinogens, analgesics, or opioids. Over half the patients in both groups reported serious signs of dependence: using to ease a hangover along with a history of tremors. Loss of control (using more than planned) was acknowledged by 90 percent of the patients.

Treatment Stays

These samples represent a very high rate of treatment completion (92 percent of Group One and 97 percent of Group Two)— in part, this is a result of study methods. Only those patients who spent a minimum of five to ten days in treatment were asked to grant consent for follow-up. This would assure they had the lucidity required for truly voluntary consent. As a result, patients who left treatment in the first week or so are excluded from the study samples: more than half of the patients who left against staff advice did so during the first week. Considering the total population of patients admitted to treatment at the participating centers, the aggregate treatment completion rate was 81 percent. Consequently, the follow-up samples are biased in favor of those who complete

Does Your Program Measure Up?

TABLE 10.2
SUBSTANCE USE FREQUENCY DURING THE YEAR PRECEDING TREATMENT

		Group 1 N=1,001	Group 2 N=2,303			
SUBSTANCE		**Not used** %	**Less than once a month** %	**1-3 times a month** %	**Weekly** %	**Daily** %
ALCOHOL	Group 1	2.5	7.0	9.7	34.6	46.1
	Group 2	4.7	4.8	8.2	30.3	52.0
MARIJUANA	Group 1	66.1	8.2	6.0	7.4	12.2
	Group 2	62.3	9.3	6.0	8.2	14.3
COCAINE	Group 1	80.9	10.4	3.7	2.8	2.2
	Group 2	76.7	11.6	4.5	3.9	3.2
STIMULANTS	Group 1	84.1	7.2	3.4	2.8	2.6
	Group 2	80.0	8.1	5.2	3.2	3.6
SEDATIVES	Group 1	88.1	4.6	3.0	1.2	3.1
	Group 2	85.6	6.2	2.8	2.2	3.1
MINOR TRANQUILIZERS	Group 1	83.1	5.1	3.6	3.0	5.1
	Group 2	80.4	7.4	4.4	3.0	4.8
HALLUCINOGENS	Group 1	91.3	6.5	1.1	0.7	0.4
	Group 2	92.1	6.7	0.7	0.4	0.1
SYNTHETIC ANALGESICS	Group 1	92.8	3.7	1.3	0.8	1.3
	Group 2	90.6	4.7	1.7	1.3	1.7
OPIOIDS	Group 1	91.9	3.2	1.9	0.7	2.2
	Group 2	90.7	4.7	1.6	1.4	1.7

treatment. Also compounding the bias is that those who complete treatment are more easily reached for interviews.

The typical treatment stay for the follow-up samples was four weeks. Longer stays were more common in Group Two which probably reflects the greater diversity of programs in this larger sample. The participation of family members was equally common in both samples with 85 to 90 percent of the patients having at least one family member involved in the treatment process. This high rate of family participation is also a result of sample selection. The aggregate rate for the intake population is 78 percent, indicating that treatment dropout and lack of family involvement are interrelated.

Abstinence After Treatment

The goal for all programs monitored by CATOR is for clients to achieve total abstinence from alcohol and other non-medically-indicated drugs following treatment. All outcome information is based on interviews with patients (or in 10 percent of the cases, with significant others designated on the consent form). The veracity of patient self-report may be questioned—this issue will be briefly addressed later in the chapter.

Table 10.3 shows some remarkable similarities in the outcome findings for the two patient groups. During any one of the four six-month follow-up periods, roughly three-fourths of the patients reported total abstinence. For the entire first year after treatment, two-thirds of both groups claimed total abstinence. And for the combined two-year follow-up period, 58 percent of Group One and close to 57 percent of Group Two reported total abstinence.

In addition to the patients who maintained total abstinence for the two-year follow-up period of this study, many others also had lengthy periods of abstinence, interrupted by only brief relapse intervals. Patients who reported any alcohol or other drug use during a six-month follow-up period were divided into two groups:

- those who had at least three consecutive months of abstinence
- those with shorter periods of abstinence or none at all

Table 10.3 shows this breakdown for both groups of patients.

A phenomenon that is consistent between groups is also reflected in these results. Although the proportion reporting abstinence for any one of the four follow-up intervals

TABLE **10.3**

ABSTINENCE AFTER TREATMENT

Group 1 N=1,001	*Group 2* N=2,303				
SIX-MONTH FOLLOW-UP PERIODS					
Months of Abstinence	**Sample**	**First**	**Second**	**Third**	**Fourth**
0-2	Group 1	8.8%	14.9%	16.9%	17.2%
	Group 2	8.8%	16.8%	17.3%	18.5%
3-5	Group 1	16.8%	10.2%	8.9%	6.8%
	Group 2	15.0%	9.9%	9.6%	7.6%
6	Group 1	74.4%	74.9%	74.2%	76.0%
	Group 2	76.2%	73.3%	73.1%	73.9%
ONE- AND TWO-YEAR FOLLOW-UP PERIODS					
Months of Abstinence	**Sample**	**First Year**	**Second Year**	**Two year Composite**	
0-2 months out of each 6	Group 1	18.3%	23.5%	28.2%	
	Group 2	19.9%	23.7%	29.3%	
3-5 months our of each 6	Group 1	15.5%	8.1%	13.8%	
	Group 2	14.6%	9.8%	14.0%	
Total abstinence	Group 1	66.2%	68.4%	58.0%	
	Group 2	65.5%	66.5%	56.7%	

remains remarkably consistent (73-76 percent), the number of patients with short relapses decreased over time, while the number with longer relapses (or continuous use), increased. During the first six months after treatment, approximately two-thirds of the patients who reported any use at all, reported at least three consecutive months of sobriety, while only one-third of the users had minimal sobriety. By the fourth contact, however, this relationship between brief relapses and prolonged relapses was inverted, with over two-thirds of those acknowledging use reporting prolonged relapse periods or continuous use versus only one-third with brief relapses.

LIMITATIONS OF FINDINGS

Threats to internal validity of results need to be addressed. Since treatment success is usually defined in terms of abstinence, we will discuss sobriety statistics in the pages that follow. Many of the general arguments are, however, applicable beyond this single dimension of recovery.

Two relevant issues in follow-up surveys are *selection bias* and *attrition.*

Selection Bias

Some factors in selection bias were described earlier. Bias was introduced in procedures that prohibited asking patients to complete a "history" and to consent to follow-up interviews until they had been in treatment for at least five days: 15 percent of the patients left treatment before completing the history. The rationale for this procedure was sound and based on ethical concerns. The waiting period was required to ensure that a patient was alcohol or drug free, and thus was clear-minded and fully capable of granting truly informed consent. Still, excluding from the study patients who left treatment in this early phase eliminated those at highest risk for relapse. So selection bias exists to the extent that the early dropouts have demographic characteristics, backgrounds, environmental conditions, or substance use histories that distinguish them from patients who remained in treatment beyond this initial period.

A second element of selection bias arises from the consent process itself. But the consent rate was extremely high for patients who completed the history form (97 percent), and refusal to grant consent did not contribute to the bias already introduced by early discharges. Considered together, 17 percent of the total sample was excluded because of early discharge from treatment or refusal to consent.

Selection bias, of course, is not unique to chemical dependency treatment outcome studies. Such bias is present in all formal research, even tightly controlled experimental designs involving random assignment of patients. Persons who volunteer to participate in such studies do not represent the population as a whole. In addition, all studies have exclusion criteria and, frequently, persons excluded are those with the poorest prognosis. Selection bias, then, does not in itself invalidate study results when its effects are taken into consideration.

Attrition

Attrition, another key threat to internal validity, is the loss of patients to follow-up. This factor can also be called *contact bias*. The follow-up sample in Group One represents 53 percent of the patients who entered treatment at the participating centers during the first study period and consented to follow-up. The follow-up sample for Group Two represents only 37 percent of its respective aggregate treatment population. Therefore, the patients located for four consecutive interviews are not a representative sample of their respective treatment groups.

Specifically, patients excluded from the follow-up samples were more likely to be young, unmarried, unemployed, and undereducated, with a history of poly-drug use and previous treatment for chemical dependency. When the follow-up samples are examined for the significance of these factors, age (under thirty), unemployment, drug use, and prior treatment are each associated with relapse to a great degree. Consequently, we can certainly state that the follow-up samples are biased toward more favorable outcomes. The question then becomes, biased to what degree? Or, to be specific, to what extent has the sample bias elevated sobriety rates beyond the "true" rate for the entire treatment population.

Before responding to this question, another internal validity issue must be addressed. This is called *response bias*. In outcome studies, participants may respond in socially desirable ways: trying to "look good" or to please the interviewer. Regarding chemical dependency treatment outcome studies, the issue of validity of patient self-reports has been researched extensively, more so than with other illnesses because denial of substance use is intrinsic to the disease process itself. Although a discussion of validity of self-report is beyond the scope of this chapter, an extensive review details the conclusions of many studies.

> The overriding conclusion based on the published literature is that alcohol abusers' [who have received treatment] self-reports are generally reliable and valid. (Sobell and Sobell 1986)

The key points regarding response bias are

- it can be minimized by attention to interview procedures
- it can be measured by using a convergent validity approach by contacting others to confirm the patients' responses

CATOR used procedures to accomplish these ends. Centralized follow-up eliminates the patient's desire to please treatment center staff and ensures his or her confidentiality. Along the same vein, trained interviewers with no personal investment in the patient's progress are less likely to exhibit demand characteristics. Finally, objective, behaviorally oriented questions elicit more honest answers than questions that are judgmental in tone or content.

To measure the veracity of patient responses after treatment, CATOR contacted a random sample of significant others. For 87 percent of the cases in which a patient reported total abstinence for a follow-up period, the confirming source gave an identical report. Furthermore, agreement rates between patients and confirming sources were comparable for nonsensitive areas such as physician office visits. While there is room for challenges to the validity of significant others' responses, these results suggest that outcome rates based solely on patient responses are inflated, although not to the extent some critics suggest.

Problems of bias cannot be solved completely because of the unknowns involved, but methods can be used to reasonably estimate outcomes for patients excluded from the follow-up sample.

- One technique is to examine outcome results for patients who were contacted for one to three interviews, and then to extrapolate abstinence rates based on declines in outcomes associated with fewer contacts. Since the relationship of number of contacts to abstinence rate is a fairly linear one, an estimate can be included for patients with no contacts.

- Another technique is to compare the characteristics of patients interviewed with those not located, and then estimate the outcome for patients not contacted based on the prognosis associated with a given characteristic or set of characteristics in the patients interviewed.

Detailing the procedures of these two techniques is not practical here. But (1) employing a combination of these two techniques, (2) factoring in an adjustment for inflated self-reported abstinence, and (3) using conservative assumptions lead us to believe that the best estimate for the true abstinence rate for the entire population admitted to treatment is 20 percent to 25 percent lower than that based on patient self-report in the follow-up sample for any given interval. Using this figure for adjustment would mean that

- At least half of all patients admitted to treatment were totally abstinent from alcohol and other drugs during any six-month period during the first two years after treatment.
- More than 40 percent were totally abstinent for the first year after treatment.
- At least one-third were totally abstinent for at least two full years after treatment.

Even though we believe these to be conservative estimates of actual outcome, they still allow more optimism than treatment doomsayers suggest.

Total continuous abstinence is not the only criterion for treatment success, nor is it necessarily the most appropriate. Many people experience a slip or relapse without adverse consequences and then return to abstinence. When treatment outcome is measured as total abstinence versus return to substance use, people who have brief relapses or who use with no adverse consequences are classified as treatment failures. In reality, outcomes are more diverse than simple success-versus-failure dichotomies, although these are the easiest to present statistically.

In recent follow-up efforts, CATOR has added questions

about consequences of use in an ongoing effort to provide increasingly sophisticated evaluations of treatment efficacy. These measures, along with measures of psychosocial functioning and use of recovery maintenance resources, can be used to assess recovery in a broader context.

EVALUATING OTHER POST-TREATMENT ASPECTS

Since alcohol and other drug abuse have such a deleterious effect on all areas of functioning, it is reasonable to expect patients' quality of life to improve following treatment. Documenting such improvements is expected of chemical dependency researchers, although the realistic limits of treatment's effects are rarely questioned. For instance, the efficacy of treatment for tuberculosis is not measured in terms of improved marital relationships, enhanced vocational functioning, or civic contributions, even when the disease has severely stressed personal relationships and constricted psychosocial growth. The same can be said even for disorders typically covered under "mental health benefits" packages by third-party providers. The treatment of depression, for instance, is not held to the same level of "proof" of benefit as is treatment for alcohol and other drug problems. Nevertheless, good arguments can be made for evaluating outcome measures beyond recovery and relapse.

Hospitalization

One important area where CATOR has consistently noted dramatic improvements is reduction of medical care following treatment. Decreases in prevalence and length of hospitalization are especially important because of the high costs associated with inpatient care. In the year following treatment, the number of patients who reported a hospitalization for medical reasons decreased by half compared with the year prior to treatment. Although the rate increased slightly in the second year after treatment compared with year one, the proportion hospitalized compared with the year before treatment was still low (55 percent for Group One in this study and 59 percent for Group Two). Lengths of stay reflected proportionate declines.

Obviously, regression to the mean can be expected to

account for some reduction in levels of medical care after treatment. *Statistical regression* refers to the tendency for abnormally high values to return to more average values over time, regardless of intervention. Many persons enter chemical dependency treatment because of deteriorating health, and some are referred directly to treatment from hospitalizations for medical or psychiatric care. Thus, their pre-treatment levels will be unusually high. Also, because many patients receive quality medical care in conjunction with chemical dependency treatment, this care may preclude the need for medical care in the months after treatment.

Despite these realities, several factors argue against attributing the dramatic declines in medical care to regression to the mean. Hospitalization rates stay low, even in the second year. Most importantly, post-treatment hospitalization rates rose over time for patients who returned to alcohol or other drug use, but remained low or continued to decline for those who remained abstinent. This significant association between alcohol and other drug use and medical care supports the hypothesis that treatment causes reduction in medical care following treatment. CATOR findings in this regard are not isolated; other studies have also documented similar patterns (Holder et al. 1985; Jones and Vischi 1979; Sherman et al. 1979).

Job Problems

Another area where significant post-treatment declines occurred was in job problems. Whereas approximately one-third of patients experienced job performance problems during the year before treatment, and at least as many reported absences from work related to their use, only very small proportions (about 3 percent) reported similar problems following treatment. Since the decline in job problems was even greater proportionately than the decrease in substance use, it is reasonable to surmise that even those patients who relapsed moderated their use to the extent that the negative impact on their job had been lessened compared with before treatment.

Arrests

Arrest frequencies showed a similar dramatic decline. In

the CATOR studies, there was a significant difference in pre-treatment arrest rates between Group One and Group Two. Including all felony and misdemeanor arrests, 22 percent of Group One and 33 percent of Group Two were arrested during the year before treatment. Following treatment, 7 percent of Group One and 13 percent of Group Two reported an arrest during the first year, and 11 percent of Group One and 12 percent of Group Two reported an arrest during year two. For both groups, the number citing two or more arrests during either year after treatment did not exceed 3 percent. Although regression to the mean is also a factor to be considered here, a marked relationship between post-treatment substance use and arrests made it reasonable to argue that treatment is a factor in the reduction in arrest rates.

Emotional Distress

Comparisons from one final area can be presented in this discussion of treatment outcome. High numbers of patients in both Group One and Group Two reported a variety of emotional distress indicators for the year before treatment. Proportions reporting frequent difficulties ranged from a low in both groups for sleep problems (46 percent of Group One and 54 percent of Group Two) to highs for tension (67 and 77 percent) and feelings of depression (66 and 77 percent). During the two years after treatment, sleep problems were reported by no more than 31 percent of the patients in either group during either one-year period; depression was reported by, at most, 45 percent and tension by, at most, 53 percent. The existence of emotional distress before treatment does not significantly affect post-treatment abstinence; however, emotional distress after treatment was associated with continued use or resumption of use of alcohol or other drugs. Levels of emotional discomfort may be related to alcohol and other drug use in several ways. Emotional discomfort may trigger using alcohol or other drugs in a misguided effort at self-medication. Alternatively, relapse to substance use may increase emotional distress since tension, depression, and sleep problems can all be direct effects of substance abuse. Another possibility is an interaction between emotional distress and substance use leading to elevated levels of distress.

Summary of Findings

Considered together, reductions in hospitalizations, job problems, arrests, and emotional distress after treatment add more weight to reported levels of abstinence as evidence of the beneficial impact of treatment. Surpassing the primary objective of helping patients to achieve freedom from their dependence on alcohol and other drugs, treatment also leads to improvements in other areas that directly benefit the patients themselves, and indirectly benefit their families and friends, their employers and co-workers, and society at large.

DIRECTIONS FOR FURTHER STUDY

CATOR has modified history questionnaires and follow-up questionnaires to more precisely measure the severity of alcohol and other drug problems. Future reports may provide more illuminating information on which substance use patterns may predict a lower likelihood of post-treatment abstinence. The continuing registry also includes more programs from more diverse areas of the country, and the impact of widespread cocaine abuse will be measurable in future studies. CATOR is also monitoring a variety of program types, including outpatient programs of differing lengths and intensity, as well as more innovative programming strategies such as combining short-term inpatient stays with longer-term outpatient treatment.

Results from the CATOR system are obviously not generalizable to all programs, particularly those treating indigent patients or patients with severe physical, mental, or social deterioration. However, it is equally important to take note of the negative impact of propagating outcome results from studies with excessively high relapse rates (Edwards et al. 1977; Mosher et al. 1975; Orford et al. 1976; Pittman and Tate 1972; Wilson et al. 1978).

Although the results of one study (Edwards et al. 1977) are often cited as particularly important because the study involved an experimental design, the conclusions drawn are unwarranted since neither advice nor treatment was effective in this particular setting. And the relapse rate for both groups was 100 percent at two years (Orford et al.

1976). Even though CATOR serves self-selected treatment programs, CATOR outcome results offer a more positive perspective on treatment outcome. Such outcome rates should serve as the standard for setting base rates of treatment efficacy for future studies involving attempts at more sophisticated procedures, such as patient matching to treatment type.

SUPPORTERS OF THE CATOR STUDY

For their support in this study we thank:

- Abbott-Northwestern Hospital Chemical Dependency Treatment Programs; Minneapolis, Minnesota
- Baton Rouge Chemical Dependency Unit; Baton Rouge, Louisiana
- Baton Rouge Chemical Dependency Unit of Acadiana; Lafayette, Louisiana
- Charter Ridge Hospital Chemical Dependency Programs; Lexington, Kentucky
- Chemical Dependency Unit of South Texas; Corpus Christi, Texas
- Elmbrook Memorial Hospital Chemical Dependency Program; Brookfield, Wisconsin
- Forest City Treatment Center; Forest City, Iowa
- Fountain Lake Treatment Center; Albert Lea, Minnesota
- Frances Mahon Deaconess Hospital Chemical Dependency Center; Glasgow, Montana
- Glenbeigh Hospital of Cleveland; Cleveland, Ohio
- Glenbeigh Hospital of Rock Creek; Rock Creek, Ohio
- HealthEast Chemical Dependency Programs; St. Paul, Minnesota
- Hopedale Hall, Hopedale Medical Complex; Hopedale, Illinois
- Lutheran Memorial Hospital Family Recovery Center; Grand Island, Nebraska
- North Colorado Family Recovery Center; Greeley, Colorado
- Powell III Chemical Dependency Center, Iowa Methodist Medical Center; Des Moines, Iowa

- St. Mary's Chemical Dependency Services, Riverside Medical Center; Minneapolis, Minnesota
- Schick Shadel Hospital; Seattle, Washington
- Theda Clark Hospital Chemical Dependency Services; Neenah, Wisconsin
- Trinity Regional Hospital; Fort Dodge, Iowa

- Data base management provided by Michael G. Luxenberg, Ph.D., President, Professional Data Analysts, Minneapolis, Minnesota
- Computer support provided by Academic Computing Services at the University of Minnesota
- Additional support provided by Ramsey Clinic Department of Psychiatry, St. Paul, Minnesota

REFERENCES

Edwards, G. et al. "Alcoholism: A controlled trial of 'treatment' and 'advice.'" *Journal of Studies on Alcohol* 38 (1977): 1004-31.

Holder, H.D., J.G. Blose, and M.J. Gasiorowski. *Alcoholism Treatment Impact on Total Health Care Utilization and Costs: A Four-Year Longitudinal Analysis of the Federal Employees Health Benefit Program with Aetna Life Insurance Company.* Chapel Hill, N.C.: H-2, Inc., 1985.

Jones, K.R., and T.R. Vischi. "Impact of alcohol, drug abuse, and mental health treatment on medical care utilization: A review of the research literature." *Medical Care* 17 (1979): 1-82.

Mosher, V. et al. "Comparison of outcome in a 9-day and 30-day alcohol treatment program." *Journal of Studies on Alcohol* 36 (1975): 1277-81.

Orford, J., E. Oppenheimer, and G. Edwards. "Abstinence or control: The outcome for excessive drinkers two years after consultation." *Behavior Research and Therapy* 14 (1976): 409-18.

Pittman, D.J., and R.L. Tate. "A comparison of two treatment programs for alcoholics." *International Journal of Addictions* 18 (1972): 183-93.

Sherman, R.M., S. Reiffs, and A.B. Forsythe. "Utilization of medical services by alcoholics participating in an outpatient treatment program." *Alcoholism: Clinical and Experimental Research* 3 (1979): 115.

Sobell, L.C., and M.B. Sobell. "Can we do without alcohol abusers' self-report?" *The Behavior Therapist* 7 (1986): 141-46.

Wilson, A., J. White, and D.E. Lange. "Outcome evaluation of a hospital-based alcoholism treatment programme." *British Journal of Addiction* 73 (1978): 39-45.

CHAPTER ELEVEN

ADOLESCENT CHEMICAL DEPENDENCY TREATMENT OUTCOME RESEARCH

Patricia Owen, Ph.D., and
Ken C. Winters, Ph.D.

Patricia Owen is a licensed consulting psychologist and Vice President of Hazelden Services, Inc. She began her work at Hazelden in the research division and developed the outcome evaluation system for Hazelden Pioneer House, a residential rehabilitation program for adolescents and young adults. Ken Winters is the Director of the Center for Adolescent Substance Abuse, a research group studying adolescent chemical dependency, which has developed an assessment battery for adolescents.

EXISTING RESEARCH

In studies conducted on adolescent chemical dependency treatment outcome, researchers have tapped large-scale data bases. In this chapter, we examine the following four studies of this nature:

1. Drug Abuse Reporting Program (DARP)
2. Treatment Outcome Prospective Study (TOPS)
3. Pennsylvania Substance-Abuse System: Uniform Data Collection System (UDCS)
4. Chemical Abuse Treatment Outcome Registry (CATOR). This study was reviewed in Chapter Ten, but we will narrow our focus to adolescents here.

The first three of these studies are similar in that each is a collection of information about clients admitted to publicly supported agencies for chemical dependency treatment. Within each agency system, adolescents were not treated separately from adults; only their data are segregated from the adults' data. The fourth large data set (CATOR) to be discussed is treatment outcome data collected by a treatment outcome registry service.

The first three data bases represent four primary treatment modalities: therapeutic communities, drug-free outpatient programs, methadone maintenance, and detoxification programs. Since few adolescents were treated in the latter two settings, this chapter excludes discussion of them. We examine treatment outcomes of the remaining two: therapeutic communities and drug-free outpatient programs. Since some of the large data bases included data from both kinds of programs, a residential versus outpatient comparison can be made. Further, one data base includes a no-treatment (waiting list) group that permits a treatment versus no-treatment comparison.

Remember that great variability exists *within* each of the two general treatment distinctions (residential versus outpatient) considered in this chapter.

- *Residential programs* range from the traditional long-term, highly structured, confrontational programs (therapeutic communities) that developed in the 1960s, to modified versions that are much less intensive and much shorter in duration (approximately one month).
- *Drug-free outpatient programs* also vary, from a few brief crisis counseling sessions to five hours each evening for several weeks.

Another factor is that we are limited in generalizing the findings, because we can presume that outpatient programs, usually publicly supported, draw clients who have no health insurance coverage for drug treatment. Thus, outpatient programs may serve a patient population very different in background characteristics than employed, insured patients. With these points in mind, we begin by examining these studies, looking at distinctions between outcome data of residential versus outpatient treatment for chemically dependent adolescents.

Drug Abuse Reporting Program (DARP)

Numerous research reports on clients in the DARP system have been published by Sells and Simpson (1979). This data base included information from fifty-two public agencies in the United States and Puerto Rico from 1969-1973. A brief description of the clients and study results comparing outpatient and residential settings is shown in table 11.1.

In terms of the sample, residential clients were generally older and more likely to be using opioids either with or without other drugs than clients in outpatient programs. Outpatient clients tended to be users of marijuana

TABLE **11.1**

DRUG ABUSE REPORTING PROGRAM (DARP)

ADOLESCENT OUTCOME

	Outpatient	Residential
Total	2745	1222
Male	63%	63%
White	85%	71%
Under age 17	72%	46%
Nonopioid only	69%	27%
Prior drug treatment	10%	16%
Median time in treatment	108 days	90 days
Quit treatment	48%	67%
Follow-up sample[a] (76%)	158	238
Abstinence from opioids	85%	91%
Abstinence from alcohol	14%	10%
Problems related to use of alcohol	6%	6%
Abstinence from marijuana	34%	33%
Abstinence from other nonopioids	71%	76%
No arrests	80%	73%
Employed 40-60 days	41%	46%

[a] Results refer to the 2 months prior to follow-up interview.

or other nonopioids (minor tranquilizers, amphetamines, cocaine, and depressants). Outcome data reporting treatment completion and follow-up functioning revealed that one-half of the outpatients and two-thirds of the residential clients quit treatment prior to completing treatment goals. Though not illustrated in the table, proportionately more blacks than whites quit, and within the blacks and whites, older clients had higher rates of quitting.

Follow-up interviews four to six years after treatment showed high levels of abstinence from opioids and nonopioids for both the residential and outpatient clients. Use of alcohol and marijuana was high, however, so drug substitution was a problem. Clients in the outpatient programs showed the most favorable outcomes, though residential outcomes were a close second on most variables. In terms of client characteristics, the researchers found that clients with the fewest problems at the time of admission were most likely to benefit from treatment. And there was a definite link between outcome and treatment length: favorableness of outcome increased with the amount of time spent in the program.

A feature of this study was its authors' effort to correct inherent biases in the study design. Because subjects were not randomly assigned to a treatment modality, statistical corrections were incorporated into the data analysis to address the fact that those clients with "good prognosis" characteristics, such as being employed and a nonopioid user, were more likely to be treated with the outpatient modality. This statistical correction is particularly important in the DARP comparison of the no-treatment group with the treatment groups since there is reason to expect that a client self-selection bias occurred across the various groups. Based on this analysis, the no-treatment group showed much *less* favorable outcomes than the outpatient and residential treatment groups.

Treatment Outcome Prospective Study (TOPS)

The TOPS study spans clients from the years 1979 to 1981, and includes eleven outpatient and fourteen residential programs in several communities of the United States. Hubbard and his colleagues (1983, 1985) have reported extensively on these data. Adolescents composed 14 percent of the residential programs and 22 percent of the outpatient programs. Residential clients were more likely to be

- multiple drug-users
- referred from a criminal justice agency
- less likely to be in school

Outpatient clients were more likely to be

- marijuana or alcohol users
- in school
- less likely to have had prior chemical dependency treatment

TABLE 11.2
TREATMENT OUTCOME PROSPECTIVE STUDY (TOPS)
ADOLESCENT OUTCOME

AGE	Outpatient		Residential	
	Younger than 18	18-19	Younger than 18	18-19
Total	391	249	199	203
Male	64%	68%	69%	71%
White	89%	82%	82%	74%
Prior drug treatment	12%	16%	29%	23%
Legal pressure	20%	39%	39%	40%
Quit treatment	31%	36%	34%	32%
Follow-up sample	80	67	38	55
Daily alcohol use	8%	14%	16%	22%
Daily marijuana use	34%	24%	22%	24%
Weekly use of their drugs	35%	39%	42%	36%
Any drug-related problem	48%	50%	43%	48%
Full-time work	17%	26%	27%	19%
Predatory illegal acts	54%	52%	38%	33%
Suicidal thoughts or attempts	23%	22%	12%	26%

Of special significance is that most youths entering the chemical dependency treatment programs surveyed had a complex array of problems other than their drug involvement: delinquency, depression, and family problems (particularly chemical-dependency-related family problems) were frequently primarily coexisting factors.

In terms of treatment completion, approximately one-third of the clients in all programs dropped out in the first month. This was evidenced by a high dropout rate in the first week of outpatient treatment, and likewise, a high dropout rate between the second and fourth week of the residential treatment sample.

Follow-up data were collected on clients one year after their treatment. The greatest improvement was seen for younger clients in residential treatment, especially for those who stayed longer than three months. Those treated in outpatient programs did not show as much improvement as their counterparts in residential treatment. It is impossible, however, to determine from the analysis whether this was due to fewer problems before treatment, or because outpatient was less effective. When the use of various drugs is examined at a one-year follow-up survey, approximately one-third of all clients report at least weekly use of alcohol, marijuana, or other drugs. Thus, treatment effectiveness appeared to be limited, since many youths continued high levels of alcohol and marijuana use after treatment.

As in the DARP study, outcome and treatment stay were related. The youths who entered residential programs showed positive behavioral changes at the one-year follow-up among those who remained in treatment for three months or more. The data pertaining to outpatient treatment, however, were not as clear: in general, outpatient treatment of three months or longer did not appear to much improve the results.

Pennsylvania Substance-Abuse System: Uniform Data Collection System (UDCS)

UDCS is a Pennsylvania statewide data collection system for 350 treatment facilities and over fifty thousand admissions a year. Rush (1979) reported outcome data on a subsample (N=3,925) of adolescents (twelve to nineteen years old) who were treated in therapeutic communities and out-patient drug-free programs. Completion of treatment was predicted for those who had the following characteristics:

- non-multiple drug abusers
- older white adolescents
- enrollment in an educational program that sup-plemented treatment
- in treatment for the first time

Some of these defining characteristics are reflected in table 11.3.

TABLE 11.3
PENNSYLVANIA SUBSTANCE ABUSE SYSTEM
UNIFORM DATA COLLECTION SYSTEM (UDCS)
ADOLESCENT OUTCOME

AGE	Outpatient		Residential		
	Younger than 18	18-19	Younger than 18	18-19	
Total	2417	1360	503	458	
Male	55%	70%	70%	59%	
White	87%	81%	88%	80%	
Nonopioid only	64%	50%	75%	45%	
Multiple drug user	47%	51%	76%	59%	
Prior drug treatment	15%	27%	36%	45%	
Legal pressure	17%	29%	44%	44%	
Median age first use	14.3	14.9	13.1	14.1	
Median time in treatment	123 days	100 days	36 days	34 days	
Quit treatment		(Proportion not given)			
Follow-up sample	1810	1186	487	442	
Productivity					
Education					
Employment		(Proportion not given)			
Arrests					
Treatment Completion					

Length of treatment was also related, but only for those in the outpatient group. Treatment outcome was primarily defined according to an index of productivity (for example, being in school, in a training program, or employed) at time of *discharge*. Time spent in treatment was the most accurate predictor of clients' productivity at discharge. There was some contradiction, however: time in treatment was *negatively* related to the productivity for those treated in an outpatient setting, but was *positively* related to productivity for clients treated in therapeutic communities. Other variables predicted the productivity outcome measure (such as number of arrests during treatment), but because the two separate treatment groups were characterized by systematic pre-treatment client differences, there is no opportunity to evaluate differential predictors of treatment effectiveness.

Chemical Abuse Treatment Outcome Registry (CATOR)

Harrison and Hoffmann (1987) reported preliminary outcome findings on a sample of 493 residentially treated adolescent clients who were contacted both at six months and twelve months (see table 11.4). The sample of contacted clients represents 54 percent of the eligible sample who had been in the registry and out of treatment for at least a year.

The detailed client profile described in the 1987 CATOR report indicates that in addition to chemical involvement, a typical client experiences multiple problems that may include

- school expulsion or suspension
- learning disability
- parental abuse of chemicals
- physical and sexual abuse
- low self-esteem
- depression
- delinquency or criminal behavior

Substance use history data indicate that alcohol and marijuana are the most frequently used substances, with marijuana preferred for daily use.

The CATOR data indicate a treatment completion rate of over two-thirds of the sample, with girls more likely

TABLE 11.4
CHEMICAL ABUSE TREATMENT OUTCOME REGISTRY (CATOR)
ADOLESCENT OUTCOME

	Residential
Total	1824
Male	67.3%
Average age	15.9%
Prior alcohol or other drug treatment	27.2%
Legal difficulties	55.0%
Median age first use: alcohol	12.1
Median age first use: other drugs	13.1
Median time in treatment	38 days
Parental substance abuse	55.0%
Did not complete treatment	31.5%
Follow-up sample[a]	493
Total abstinence	43.6%
Brief relapse	22.5%
Multiple relapse	33.9%

[a] Consists of those who were out of treatment for a year (915) and for whom interviews were completed at both the 6-month and 12-month contact points.

than boys to complete treatment (75 percent versus 66 percent). Boys were much more likely to be discharged for behavioral problems. In terms of treatment outcome, less than half (43.6 percent) of the sample reported total abstinence for the full year after completion of residential treatment. Girls, as a whole, reported more abstinence than boys (50 percent versus 40 percent). The proportion of boys and girls assigned to the brief relapse category (at least three to five months of sobriety) was roughly equal (total of 22.5 percent), but boys were found to more likely report prolonged or multiple relapses than girls (26 percent versus 39 percent).

Analyses were conducted to identify pre-treatment and outcome correlates. For girls, a suicide attempt, legal problems, physical abuse by a family member, serious school problems, or depressive-like symptoms were each associated with a greater likelihood of relapse. When correlates for boys were examined, there was a clear trend for legal problems and a inflated self-concept to be linked with a greater probability of relapse. (Harrison and Hoffmann hypothesize that the self-concept variable may be related to denial of problems and motivation to change; that is, those with a *low* self-concept may not minimize their problems and may be more motivated to change.)

The key variable that was demonstrated as the best predictor of post-treatment abstinence was regular attendance at AA or other support groups.

Smaller Studies

Two Scandinavian studies of young drug abusers have identified client characteristics that influence treatment outcome. Holsten (1980) found that 26 percent of the variance in outcome at one to six years after treatment was associated with the following characteristics:

- the youth not being registered for criminality during the twelve months prior to the first contact
- no alcohol problems at the time of the first contact
- being female
- being raised in a broken home
- having a father who had no alcohol problems during the youth's childhood

Benson (1985) found that continued users after treatment tended to

- deviate more from school careers
- be more truant if they were male
- have one or more alcoholic parents if they were female

Low intensity of drug and inhalant abuse following treatment were positive prognostic factors.

Vaglum and Fossheim (1980) reported that adolescents' responses to various forms of treatment depended on their primary drug of abuse. For users of psychedelic drugs, family therapy, followed by individual psychotherapy, was most positively correlated with outcome, whereas con-

frontational milieu therapy was slightly negatively correlated with outcome. Conversely, for opioid and central nervous system stimulant users, the degree of confrontational
milieu therapy was directed toward a positive outcome,
followed by family therapy and individual psychotherapy.

Finally, Owen (1984) reported preliminary findings from
a residential adolescent treatment program in Minnesota
(Hazelden Pioneer House). Treatment completion was quite
good: 75 percent completed the one-month program. Six-
month follow-up data on 144 adolescent clients (45 percent
of the eligible sample) indicated that 67 percent reported
total abstinence from both alcohol and other drugs.

Reaching Some Conclusions

The studies reviewed here, despite their methodological
flaws, offer us an initial view of the state of adolescent
treatment outcome. In general, three tentative conclusions
can be made: (1) some treatment is probably better than
none; (2) factors and variables have been identified that
appear to be associated with treatment completion and
relapse; and (3) there is no satisfactory evidence to prove
that different treatment modalities show differential
effects. With respect to this last point, residential clients
were more often associated with poorer outcome in some of
the studies. Yet, because such clients often have more *poor
prognosis* characteristics (including legal problems, being
male, prior treatment history) than outpatient clients, we
cannot make equitable comparisons between the two treatment modalities.

The results across the studies show room for improvement in terms of treatment effectiveness. Drop-out rates
were reported to be relatively variable and high across
treatments. These rates were as high as 67 percent in the
DARP sample and as low as 26 percent (females) in the
CATOR sample. In terms of post-treatment functioning,
non-sobriety rates, measuring use over a period of up to
twelve months, have been reported to be at or over 50 percent in some of the studies (CATOR and DARP).

Some factors appear to be associated with treatment outcome. At the top of the next page are two treatment variables that appear to show a relationship to good outcome.

- length of stay in treatment
- involvement in a post-treatment support group

It is also becoming clearer which client variables may be linked to poor outcome. These include being

- young
- male
- uneducated
- non-white
- an opioid user with a criminal history

These clients likely need more specialized and intensive services if we expect to improve their treatment outcomes.

RESEARCH ISSUES

There are several issues to consider when planning and implementing adolescent treatment outcome studies. Overall, research studies indicate that adolescents in treatment differ from adults in many ways. Adolescents are likely to be poly-drug users (Winters in press[a]). Their pattern of substance use may be more similar to adolescents in general (those not in treatment) than to their adult counterparts in treatment (Pandina and Raskin 1981). Use of marijuana and alcohol is particularly common, with cocaine becoming more prevalent.

Adolescents differ from adults in that they often experience more distress in their family of origin and may be victims of sexual and physical abuse. Also, many are more likely to be referred to treatment by family or other agencies, rather than to seek treatment on their own behalf Motivation may therefore be lower, and the intent to minimize problems may be greater.

In treatment, adolescents may present a myriad of developmental and psychiatric problems beyond those problems normally associated with alcohol or other drug abuse among adults. This is illustrated by the findings from the TOPS researchers that showed high rates of symptoms of depression and histories of suicide ideation and attempts. Similar data were reported by CATOR.

The concept of *developmental lag* is often used to describe many of the social and emotional problems among adolescent drug abusers. Baumrind, Moselle, and Martin (1985) admirably describe components and causes of this phenomenon from a theoretical point of view. They discuss how alcohol and other drug use may adversely interact with the adolescent's difficulty in becoming proficient in formal cognitive tasks, and in relinquishing illusions of egocentricity and achieving normal emancipation from his or her family of origin. Since most chemically dependent adults in treatment have made some headway in these areas, there is usually little need to incorporate such topics into their treatment plans. For adolescents, however, these areas may play a crucial role in treatment outcome.

Another difference between adolescents and adults is that youths leave treatment and return to environments over which they have little control. Many are discharged into a family and a peer group that have probably not changed much, if any, since the teenager left, so many of the environmental stimuli for drug use remain intact. Consequently, compared to adult clients, adolescents may not be able to exert as much change over the type or amount of interaction they have with people around them after treatment. Also, many more adolescents than adults are referred to institutional environments (for example, halfway houses or training schools) after primary treatment. This is an added dimension to consider in terms of treatment composition and interpretation of outcome results.

Effects of Health Care Trends

Additional health care trends must be faced in making recommendations for future research into adolescent treatment.

- First, third-party payors are demanding less treatment, in the form of either outpatient treatment or in shorter inpatient treatment. For example, Blue Cross and Blue Shield of Minnesota determined that for 1981, 19 percent of juvenile chemical dependency days for which it received claims were "medically unnecessary" (Jackson-Beeck 1983). This finding was roughly equivalent to its decision for adults in chemical dependency treatment during the same time period. Health maintenance organizations are rapidly growing in all states and currently have enrollments from 10 to 42 percent of people in eight states and the District of Columbia (*Hospitals* 1985). The growth of HMOs and preferred provider arrangements, with strong emphasis on cost containment, is likely to bring pressure to treatment centers to conform to external standards of treatment composition, variables measured, and length of stay.

- A second consideration comes from the juvenile justice system (Schwartz et al. 1984; Krisberg and Schwartz 1983). In 1974, the Juvenile Justice and Delinquency Prevention Act was signed. Among other things, this act stipulated that status offenders (runaways, truants, children in conflict with parents) could no longer be incarcerated. At that time, nearly 40 percent of youths in criminal justice institutions were being held for status offenses. Current concerns are that many of these youths are being erroneously placed in chemical dependency treatment centers and psychiatric institutions. Consequently, lobbying efforts are in progress to change or limit inpatient placement of adolescents for alcohol or other drug abuse, and/or to require demonstration of the need for and effectiveness of inpatient treatment, as opposed to outpatient treatment. Suggested modifications include independent prospective external review of admissions, court involvement for most or all youths to determine appropriateness of setting, segregation of adolescents in treatment from adults, and expanded use of standardized assessment measures and procedures (Winters in press[b]).

- A third factor to consider is the growing push within the educational and health care systems to identify and refer teenagers who show early signs of drug abuse. This call for expanding the detection and prevention-treatment network is motivated by society's recent perception that teenage drug involvement is a great public health concern. If more and varied youth at earlier ages are being identified as needing evaluation or treatment services, it will be important for researchers to clearly define the types of teenagers and services included in their studies.

These general issues create a heightened interest in demonstrating the effectiveness of treatment for adolescent chemical involvement. Expansion of services is costly; pressure to expand the "detection systems" can lead to unfortunate abuses if youth are inappropriately diagnosed and referred. It is imperative that treatment centers and researchers in the area of adolescent alcohol and other drug abuse take a proactive stance in determining the factors associated with successful treatment.

Specific Considerations

We recommend the following considerations for those conducting future research in adolescent treatment outcome:

1. *Use smaller samples to facilitate better methodology.* While large-scale studies using national data bases, as described in this chapter, have been exceedingly helpful to many people in beginning to understand the nature of adolescent alcohol and other drug abuse treatment, focus on smaller-scale studies would be better. In smaller studies, the measurement and manipulation of variables can be more easily controlled and interpreted.
2. *Adhere to high standards of research methodology.* Future outcome research needs better explanation of how samples and subjects were selected, the diagnostic groupings for subjects (with regard to substance abuse and dependence as well as other disorders), better demographic descriptions of the subjects, and clear explanation of follow-up methods and responses rates.
3. *Describe the components of treatment for which outcomes are being reported.* As noted in this chapter, the comparison between the modalities of residential and outpatient treatment is usually artificial because the *within-modality* differences are as large or larger than the *between-modality* differences. Treatment components are the pieces

of the total treatment package, whether residential or outpatient, and may include activities such as individual counseling, group therapy, or didactic lectures. Also, the components of adolescent treatment may be quite different from the components of adult treatment because of the unique characteristics of adolescents. For example, adolescent treatment components may include daily school, vocational testing and counseling, as well as recreation and parent education. Theoretically, some residential and outpatient programs may have the same components.

4. *Describe the treatment philosophy guiding the treatment program.* Generally, treatment components are infused with a dominating treatment philosophy. For example, in a program based on Alcoholics Anonymous or Narcotics Anonymous, much time would be spent on the Twelve Step program in counseling sessions. The creators of programs based on a psychiatric model may view adolescent drug use as a symptom, and design the content of treatment components to address emotional problems, limiting discussions about drug use. We know very little about the variations on treatment philosophy and their effects on outcome.

5. *Describe the intensity of treatment.* While this includes variables such as time spent in the various components (such as number of hours of group counseling per day), it also includes aspects that are more difficult to quantify, such as the average staff-to-patient ratio, the amount of the day that is structured, and expectations for patients in the treatment program.

6. *Describe the aftercare setting or post-treatment environment to which the adolescent is being referred.* A large proportion of adolescents are placed in halfway houses, foster care, or training schools after treatment, while others may be referred to occasional counseling or involvement in self-help groups in their home community. Just as primary treatment settings vary in components and intensity, so do post-treatment settings. Outcomes are best interpreted with these differences in mind.

7. *Measure post-treatment use of alcohol and all other drugs, rather than one particular type of drug or class of drugs.* Previous research shows that adolescents who are admitted to treatment with a primary pattern of opioid and nonopioid drug use are likely to report a continuing or increasing pattern of alcohol and marijuana use after treatment. Most people who interpret treatment outcome studies would not view this as favorable.

8. *Report the proportion of clients at outcome who are totally abstinent.* A study of young adults, not reviewed in this chapter, illustrates this point well (Coombs 1978). In this outcome study of 265 therapeutic community clients, the usual univariate single categories of drug use rates are reported. For example, 82 percent of one sub-group were abstinent from opioids, 18 percent were abstinent from alcohol, and so forth. In the final treatment analysis, however, only 4.3 percent were abstinent from *all* substances. The reporting of combined alcohol and other drug use figures is helpful in interpreting study results.

9. *Supplement use of the self-report method with laboratory tests.* Sole reliance on self-report can inflate abstinence rates and thus encourage misleading conclusions about outcome. Urinalysis is fairly inexpensive, and laboratory procedures are more standardized so that high accuracy of results can be expected.

10. *State the expected criteria for successful outcome.* Much work needs to be done in this area, since there appears to be little published description of what constitutes good outcome among adolescents. Presumably, criteria for successful treatment will vary somewhat with treatment philosophy. Nonetheless, when outcome goals are not clearly stated, it is impossible to determine whether treatment was effective.

11. *Report correlations between alcohol use, other drug use, emotional stability, social functioning and legal, educational, or employment status.* First, although there is reason to believe that abstinence at follow-up correlates positively with satisfactory

or improved functioning in other areas, no data in the adolescent outcome literature either refute or support this. Second, because adolescents are even more likely than their adult counterparts to display developmental problems, the existence or resolution of these problems needs to be examined.

More Research Is Needed

In sum, we need much more research in the area of adolescent chemical dependency treatment. Because this area is in its infancy, even small, descriptive studies of clients, treatment, and outcomes would be helpful. We will, however, ultimately need research that goes beyond simple dichotomous reports of use or non-use of chemicals, or presence or absence of related problems after treatment. Future research will need to use experimental designs and multivariate analyses to help clinicians answer the complex questions about how to continue to make treatment effective for adolescents.

REFERENCES

Author. "Baby boomers help HMOs grow to 42 states." *Hospitals* 59 (1985): 88-89.

Baumrind, D., K. Moselle, and J. Martin. "Adolescent drug research: A critical examination from a developmental perspective." *Advances in Alcohol and Substance Abuse* 3-4 (1985): 41-67.

Benson, G. "Course and outcome of drug abuse and medical and social condition in selected young abusers." *Acta Psychiatrica Scandinavian* 71 (1985): 48-66.

Coombs, R.H. "Back on the streets: Therapeutic communities' impact upon drug users." *American Journal of Drug and Alcohol Abuse* 8 (1978):185-201.

Harrison, P.A., and N. Hoffmann. CATOR 1987 Report: Adolescent Residential Treatment Intake and Follow-Up Findings. St. Paul, Minn.: CATOR, 1987.

Holsten, F. "Repeat follow-up studies of 100 young Norwegian drug abusers." *Journal of Drug Issues* 10 (1980): 491-504.

Hubbard, R.L. et al. "Alcohol use and problems among adolescent clients in drug treatment programs." *Alcohol Health and Research World* (1983): 10-18.

Hubbard, R.L. et al. "Characteristics, behaviors and outcomes for youth in the TOPS." In *Treatment Services for Adolescent Substance Abusers.* Rockville, Md.: National Institute of Drug Abuse, 1985.

Jackson-Beeck, M. *Effective Care '81 Program Status Report.* Minneapolis: Blue Cross and Blue Shield of Minnesota, 1983.

Krisberg, B., and I. Schwartz. "Rethinking juvenile justice." *Crime and Delinquency* (July 1983): 333-64.

Owen, P. "Outcome of adolescents in chemical dependency treatment." Center City, Minn.: Hazelden Foundation, 1984.

Pandina, R.J., and H.R. White. "Patterns of alcohol and drug use of adolescent students and adolescents in treatment." *Journal of Studies on Alcohol* 42 (1981): 441-56.

Rush, T.V. "Predicting treatment outcomes for juvenile and young-adult clients in the Pennsylvania substance-abuse system." Eds., G.M. Beschner and A.S. Friedman. In *Youth Drug Abuse: Problems, Issues, and Treatment.* Lexington, Mass.: Lexington Books, 1979.

Schwartz, I.M., M. Jackson-Beeck, and R. Anderson. "The 'hidden' system of juvenile control." *Crime and Delinquency* 30 (1984): 371-85.

Sells, S.B., and D.D. Simpson. "Evaluation of treatment outcome for youths in drug abuse reporting program (DARP): A follow-up study." Ed., G.M. Beschner and A.S. Friedman. In *Youth drug abuse: Problems, Issues, and Treatment.* Lexington, Mass.: Lexington Books, 1979.

Vaglum, P., and I. Fossheim. "Differential treatment of young abusers: A quasi-experimental study of a 'therapeutic community' in a psychiatric hospital." *Journal of Drug Issues* 10 (1980): 505-16.

Winters, K.C.[a] "Clinical considerations in the assessment of adolescent chemical dependency." *Journal of Adolescent Chemical Dependency.*

Winters, K.C.[b] "The need for improved assessment of adolescent substance involvement." *Journal of Drug Issues.*

CHAPTER TWELVE

COST ANALYSES OF CHEMICAL DEPENDENCY TREATMENT

Norman G. Hoffmann, Ph.D., and Jerry Spicer

No topic generates more concerned discussion among health care professionals than rising costs. Employers, third-party payors, providers, and the public have become increasingly concerned about how health care dollars are spent. The proportion of the gross national product spent on health care in the United States is one of the highest in industrialized nations. As the costs of medical care continued to rise faster than inflation and many other expenditures, employers and other payors have increasingly focused on alternatives to traditional care and other cost-limiting strategies. Although much of the attention has focused on general medical delivery systems, chemical dependency treatment programs are under increasing pressure to verify the efficacy of treatment services and to implement efforts to minimize costs.

As a result, outcome evaluation has had to range beyond clinical measures to a variety of cost analyses. This chapter examines the issues, assumptions, and implications related to cost analyses used in evaluating chemical dependency treatment programs. Most cost analyses fall into one of four general categories:

1. cost containment
2. cost effectiveness
3. cost offset (or cost impact)
4. cost benefit

Unfortunately, these concepts are often confused, and their implied assumptions and limitations are not fully appreciated. Consequently, serious errors and misinterpretations can occur in evaluating new service models and alternate delivery systems.

Before a discussion of the various cost analyses, several issues should be noted. First, the financial "bottom line" is but one measure of program success. It is impossible to attach a financial value to human life or well-being. Second, economic estimates, no matter how sophisticated, are just that—estimates. All costs directly related to chemical dependency are often difficult to measure, but the secondary or ripple effects of chemical dependency or its treatment are virtually impossible to measure with precision. In short, financial analyses and projections are fallible estimates, and they provide only one angle of the total perspective for viewing a complex phenomena.

Categories of Cost Analyses

Many people and groups are involved in examining the issues of health care costs and proposed solutions to various aspects of rising costs. Unfortunately, these groups are not all in agreement about goals, assumptions, or approaches necessary to accomplish cost control. Before some of the relevant studies in this area can be discussed, we must clarify key terms used. For an overview of these and their definitions see figure 12.1.

COST CONTAINMENT

One of the most commonly used terms is cost containment. Cost containment refers to strategies used to control the costs of providing services. Such strategies include

- utilization review to ensure that provided services are defensible
- preferred provider organizations, in which providers provide discounts for groups of clients
- prepaid, or capitation, contracts in which providers are paid on the basis of the number of individuals who are covered, so that efficiency of service is the incentive for the provider network
- wellness, or problem prevention, programs

COST-CONTAINMENT ACTIVITIES

Those strategies used to reduce expenditures or control rising costs. Typically, cost containment activities do not focus on long-term issues.

Example:

Prepaid systems, claims review, use of preferred providers, increasing deductibles.

COST OFFSET (COST IMPACT) STUDIES:

Determination of those areas where cost savings occur as a result of providing a service. Do not compare models. A dollar estimate of the savings is not required.

Example:

Showing the percentage reduction in employee absenteeism following treatment.

COST-EFFECTIVENESS STUDIES:

Calculation of the cost of obtaining some desired *outcome*. Will typically be a ratio of the cost of obtaining a result divided by the number of desired outcomes (not necessarily expressed in dollars). Can compare different ways of achieving the same objective.

Example:

Comparing inpatient and outpatient requires dividing the real costs of each by the number of improved clients.

COST-BENEFIT ANALYSIS:

A comparison of the benefits of a program with its costs. Requires consideration of all long-term and related benefits and costs. Can be used to compare very different programs.

Example:

A comparison of a community hypertension screening program with an alcoholism treatment program.

FIGURE 12.1
COST-ANALYSES TERMS

The effectiveness of cost-containment efforts is usually assessed by considering the costs for a given service over a specified time without consideration of treatment effectiveness or consequences of reducing availability of service.

The rationale for most cost-containment endeavors is that tight control of expenditures will serve to reduce costs or at least contain increases. An assumption inherent in most cost-containment efforts is that savings can be realized by eliminating waste or inefficiency in the care delivery system. Inefficiency is presumed to be due to factors such as overcharging (by at least some providers), inefficient use of available resources (by at least some providers), use of a more expensive service when a less expensive one would be adequate, and beyond these, overuse of some services by consumers. To the extent that consistent monitoring can prevent financial abuses of payment systems and promote efficiency of service delivery, cost containment can be effective in controlling treatment costs.

Many cost-containment efforts, however, have narrowed vision to short-term benefits without consideration of the long-term consequences. In such cases, so-called "cost containment" may be at best *cost deferments,* and at worst may result in greater long-term costs. To draw an analogy on a personal level, cost containment is what many of us do several days before payday—we stop writing checks. This does not mean our bills or expenses are not growing. We simply are not paying for them at that time. Deferment of costs is an illusionary savings because the bills will still have to be paid; if the delay is too long, interest may be an added cost.

In health care systems, when cost deferment results in services not being sought or provided in a timely manner, long-term costs can escalate. Just as failing to repair a minor problem on an automobile can result in major damage or even a serious accident, so a community's failure to attend to its members' minor or early health care needs can result in substantial future expenses.

Another illusionary cost-containment strategy is *cost shifting.* This involves cutting costs borne by one payor source at the expense of the others. Increasing deductibles or co-payments are examples of these strategies. In theory, such strategies are effective cost-containment approaches because the consumer is more selective and conservative in obtaining services. But, in reality, these strategies usually do not have incentives for prevention or early intervention, so they have the same limitations as cost deferment.

Effective cost-containment efforts can point to using less expensive options, more efficient delivery systems, and rigorous control and monitoring of costs. If two types of procedures or services can be used to treat the same condition, it is logical to use the less expensive. In chemical dependency treatment, such cost containment has taken the form of urging use of the least restrictive and least costly care possible. Admission, transfer, and discharge criteria have been developed to provide guidelines for such decisions (Hoffmann et al. 1987). Regulations governing length of stay and maximum reimbursements for a given treatment, service, or procedure have also been initiated in a variety of payment systems. These strategies involve direct monitoring of clinical services and are supposed to be driven by the current standards of clinical necessity.

Other attempts at cost containment include the development of health maintenance organizations (HMOs) in which the health care institution agrees to provide required services for a group of individuals on the basis of a global per-person fee. The theory is that this enables the provider to offer the most efficient service while focusing more on prevention and health maintenance efforts. At present, the success of HMOs in reducing long-term health care costs is still in question. Preferred provider organizations (PPOs) are essentially providers or networks of providers who agree to provide services at a discounted rate in exchange for some referral advantage. Unlike the direct service monitoring strategies, these approaches are management and financial innovations.

> Cost-effectiveness is the cost of achieving a given outcome for a given condition with a given type of client or patient.

Cost-containment analyses usually emphasize the extent to which service costs are reduced after implementation of cost-containment is introduced. On a long-term basis, cost-containment analyses may concentrate on the rate of cost increases and the proportion of incurred charges that are clinically defensible. In other words, cost-containment analyses focus on monitoring financial efficiency of service delivery and eliminating waste in acute-care service delivery, but they should not ignore the importance of prevention, early intervention, and maintenance services as part of the continuity of care. It is very difficult to assess the success of containment efforts due to issues of treatment efficacy, which influence cost effectiveness, and other cost issues discussed in the following sections.

COST EFFECTIVENESS

Though often confused with cost containment, cost effectiveness is a more sophisticated concept. *Cost effectiveness* is the cost of achieving a given outcome for a given condition with a given type of client or patient. In chemical dependency treatment, this could be translated into the cost of helping one individual achieve and maintain sobriety for a given length of time. Since chemical dependency is a chronic condition, not only the acute-care but also maintenance services must be considered. Unlike onetime acute-care procedures, such as an operation for appendicitis, chemical dependency—like diabetes and hypertension—is a chronic condition that must be controlled for the remainder of the person's lifetime. Thus, we must take into account both acute-care and maintenance services in computing cost effectiveness for chemical dependency treatment.

Cost-effectiveness analysis "permits comparison of cost per unit of effectiveness against competing alternatives designed to serve the same basic purpose" (Warner and Bryan 1982). The results are usually expressed as a ratio of the cost of providing a given service or program for a given group of individuals divided by the number of desired outcomes obtained for the group. The service cost is typically expressed in dollars, and the outcome measure can be expressed in desired outcome, such as persons abstinent for a given period of time or number of people still living. In this manner, the cost effectiveness of a treatment program might be judged by the cost of keeping one patient sober for a year. This cost would include not only the charges for the successful patient, but also the proportional cost for unsuccessful ones as well. For example, a program that charges

$9,000 for acute care and aftercare for one year would have a cost per success of $18,000 if half the patients stayed sober, but the cost would be $27,000 per success if only one in three patients remained abstinent.

Cost-effectiveness analysis can be used to compare different types of programs; however, it is important that the same conditions and the same types of clients are involved in both types of programs and that the programs have the same objectives. For example, with this method, outpatient and inpatient programs can be compared using abstinence as the common outcome measure. As stated, the programs being compared need to have the same types of clients; otherwise any differences could result because of differences in clients and not from differences in program effectiveness (Spicer et al. 1981).

An example of cost-effectiveness analysis is seen in figure 12.2.

Program	Treatment Cost/Client	Annual Cost	Recovery Rate*	Cost Effectiveness Ratio
A (100 clients)	$ 8,000	$ 800,000	50%	$\frac{800,000/50\% = \$16,000}{100}$
B (100 clients)	$10,000	$1,000,000	65%	$\frac{1,000,000/65\% = \$15,385}{100}$

* Percent of patients abstinent for one year.
Interpretation: Although Program A has the least costly program on a per treatment and total cost basis, Program B achieves a better positive outcome (recovery) at a lower cost. Program B therefore is a more cost-effective program.

FIGURE 12.2
COST-EFFECTIVENESS EXAMPLE

Two treatment programs, A and B, are similar in model of treatment and serve the same client population. A sample of one hundred consecutive admissions to each program is followed to assess treatment outcome. Although Program A is less expensive ($2,000 less than Program B), we can make no assumptions about cost effectiveness by knowing only the total cost of the program. But with a measure of program effectiveness, such as a one-year recovery rate, a comparison of the total cost of the program against the number of favorable outcomes will show which program is more cost effective. In this example, Program B is actually more cost effective because its higher outcome (recovery) rate results in a lower cost per recovery at one year after treatment. This example demonstrates that cost effectiveness is not synonymous with either the total cost of treatment or the cost per unit of service. Such costs are only half of the equation with the outcome criteria being the other half.

The risks in applying cost-effectiveness analysis to comparison of inpatient and outpatient services are legion. Outpatient programs typically serve a very different patient population than inpatient programs, and simply selecting matched pairs of patients ignores the context in which the individuals are treated. The characteristics of a person's patient peers in a program could possibly influence the probability of completing treatment and remaining active in aftercare or other support networks, such as AA or NA.

Another frequently overlooked issue in such comparisons is the fact that non-clinical factors, such as logistics, finances, and personal circumstance, often preclude a given type of treatment. For example, a person who lives beyond commuting distance to an outpatient program is unable to participate. We must exercise caution in using cost-effectiveness analysis to compare different types of programs, and take into consideration extraneous biases and outcome influences.

COST OFFSET (COST IMPACT)

Cost offset and *cost impact* are synonymous terms, referring to the extent to which the cost of a service is compensated, or offset, by savings in other areas.

The objective of cost-offset analyses is to determine the extent to which the costs of providing a service such as chemical dependency treatment are offset by reducing other expenses after treatment, such as costs of health care, employee absenteeism, and injuries. Although most analyses focus on monetary value, cost benefits can include reduction of accident rates, drunken driving arrests, or days of hospitalization. Cost-offset analyses usually concentrate on cost factors for the patient population rather than those of family members and others.

Unlike cost-containment analyses, which consider only costs of the service, and cost-effectiveness analyses, which require knowledge of treatment success, cost-offset analyses typically compare pre- and post-service costs of other factors with the cost of the service. While we would expect programs more effective in terms of abstinence rate to have better cost offsets, program success *per se* does not enter into this equation. For example, a program serving a late-stage population may have a low sobriety rate, but if it is able to show a substantial reduction in high-cost areas, such as medical hospitalizations, it may show a very favorable cost-offset ratio.

COST BENEFIT

Cost-benefit analyses is the most sophisticated type of economic analyses where all costs directly and indirectly related to a condition before the service, the service cost itself, and the outcome benefits are expressed in dollars (Levin 1983). The end result, or net benefit, is a monetary measure of the service's benefits minus costs. Because cost-benefit analyses results in a standardized monetary measure, very different programs can be compared (for example, a hypertension screening program may be compared with an alcoholism treatment program).

Cost-benefit analyses is similar to cost-offset analyses in that both compare benefits or savings with costs of the service. Cost-benefit analyses, however, typically cover a broader range of costs and attempt to estimate secondary costs and project savings and costs over time. Cost-benefit studies require a side scope of data from a variety of sources. The overall costs of not treating a condition must be estimated as well as the costs of treatment. Thus, for alcoholism and other drug dependencies, we must consider such areas as losses related to mortality, reduced productivity, motor vehicle and other accidents, crime related to alcohol or other drug use or procurement, and losses suffered by others as a consequence of the behaviors of chemically dependent individuals. In effect, cost-offset analyses constitute only a limited subset of cost-benefit analyses.

Since cost-benefit analyses are beyond the scope of this chapter, and the issue of treatment effectiveness has been discussed at some length, the remainder of this chapter will deal with selected cost-offset findings. Some *general* aspects of costs associated with untreated addictions will be explored.

SPECIAL ISSUES IN COST-OFFSET/COST-IMPACT ANALYSIS

Some perspective on costs may be useful before considering a few of the specific returns that may be expected from an investment in treatment. Obviously, for any given service, the proportion of costs that can be recovered from other savings is greater as the costs become smaller. The direct cost of delivering a unit of service may be substantially less than the total cost for that service. When an automobile service department bills a customer $40 per hour for labor, this does not mean that the mechanic receives $1,600 per week. The charge must cover the overhead of rent, utilities, tools and other equipment, advertising, accounting, and other expenses of doing business, in addition to the salaries and benefits of employees. The same is true for any health care service.

Although we may wish for a utopian society where the ill and afflicted are cared for, the truth is that people and organizations that provide those services expect to make a reasonable living, just as the mechanic who repairs a car or the production supervisor where the car was manufactured.

In short, health care is a business, subject to the associated costs of all businesses. Thus, it is also subject to the ultimate principles of business: few quality workers are willing to work without reasonable pay, and no business survives unless its revenues equal or exceed expenses. This is true for both nonprofit and for-profit corporations. A nonprofit corporation that consistently loses money must be supported by the government or another source and thereby *breaks even* or shows *excess revenues*. Any health care organization that fails to balance its revenues and expenses ceases to exist after several years.

Thus, in assessing treatment costs, a program must include all components that are included in the charges, or total costs. Even with close attention to cost containment and cost effectiveness, we can find substantial variations in the costs of treatment programs. Differences are due to the type of patient a given program is capable of treating, geographic differentials in the costs of providing the services, and a variety of other factors.

In summary, the term *treatment cost* as used in the remainder of this chapter refers to total cost, or treatment charges. While we do not deal with analyses of a reasonable range of treatment costs for given types of programs, we believe that this issue is best resolved through careful attention to quality of care and the pressures for cost effectiveness from the marketplace.

Costs of Not Treating Chemical Dependency

The costs of chemical dependency to our society are vast. Economists and other researchers have attempted to assess the costs of alcoholism and other chemical dependency in terms of annual costs of chemical dependency treatment, health care costs, mortality, vocational functioning and lost productivity, accidents, fires, and crime related to alcohol and other drugs (Saxe et al. 1983). One of the most recent and most thorough of such studies, based on data from 1980, estimated the costs for 1983 to be almost $117 million for alcohol and $60 million for all other drugs combined (Harwood et al. 1984). This estimate of drug costs, of course, predates the current proliferation of problems related to cocaine abuse. Of the nearly $180 billion annual cost of chemical dependency, less than $17 billion was spent on treatment and indirect support for clinical services. Thus, the vast majority of costs clearly attributable to chemical dependency are not treatment costs.

The cost projections of chemical dependency are likely to be conservative, minimal cost estimates. This is true for three reasons.

- First, not all the costs may be obvious or known. For example, one of the earlier estimates failed to consider fetal alcohol syndrome in cost estimates (Saxe et al. 1983).
- Second, a monetary loss in one area (such as a traffic accident) usually has a ripple effect (like throwing a rock in a pond), creating additional

losses to society in numerous other areas (for example, the legal system and medical system, employee absenteeism, spouse absenteeism, or care insurance premiums). These secondary costs may be difficult, if not impossible, to trace or estimate, and they may contribute to later costs. For example, not only may an individual injured by a drunk driver miss work due to convalescence, but his or her spouse may also miss work in order to provide care. Later, the individual may suffer further complications or require other services—perhaps a knee operation as a consequence of injuries originally suffered in the accident.

• Third, the losses assessed in the literature have focused specifically on documentable monetary loss. There are, however, the more intangible losses from troubled employees, such as stress and lowered morale—or the losses in families, such as poor school performance. Further, the lost opportunities of children due to the chemical dependency of others also affect a society in innumerable ways.

One of few studies that empirically demonstrate the costs of untreated alcoholism was conducted with the General Motors-United Auto Workers Substance Abuse Program (Wright 1983). One group of 102 employees who were identified as having problems related to alcohol abuse underwent treatment. A second group of 48 employees, also determined to have problems related to alcohol abuse, did not receive treatment. In the case of the first group, use of benefits resulting from sickness and accidents *decreased* by 80 percent over a two-year span following their treatment for chemical dependency. But there was an *increase* of 128 percent for benefits resulting from sickness and accidents for the second group who did not receive treatment.

Selected Studies On Cost Offset/Cost Impact

Evidence is ever increasing that providing appropriate treatment for alcoholism and other drug addictions reduces the costs associated with chemical dependency. The fact that there is some return on the investment for treatment does not appear to be disputable. The real questions, however, appear to be, how great are the returns? And are the returns sufficient to offset all the treatment costs? In other words, is there a net gain or does the cost of treatment for unsuccessful cases result in a net loss?

No other area of the health care system is under such financial standards for justification. In all other areas, humanitarian concerns appear to be sufficient justification. Organ transplants, though enormously costly, are not challenged even though the investment is unlikely to be recovered through the productivity of the individuals receiving the organs. Persons suffering from hypertension are not threatened with loss of coverage because they continue to smoke, eat too much, or fail to exercise. Yet we continue to see proposals to limit coverage for chemical dependency treatment to two treatments per an individual's lifetime because treatment is costly. Should we then not also impose limits on transplant attempts, or admissions for coronary conditions?

Financial returns from the treatment of chemical dependency may be realized in a variety of areas, just as the total costs of chemical dependency cover a wide range. While we will not discuss a comprehensive cost-benefit analysis, we will highlight a sample of areas where cost offsets are likely to be realized. Therefore, we will concentrate on areas where there are relatively direct cost associations and where reductions in costs can be documented. The two areas of focus will be in *medical costs* and *vocational functioning*. These were chosen because they represent costs that will accrue when the chemical dependency continues and because they represent the interests of treatment payors: health care insurance and employers.

EVIDENCE OF COST OFFSETS IN MEDICAL CARE UTILIZATION

An early literature review cited a number of studies showing that treatment for chemical dependency can result in reductions in total medical care use (Jones and Vischi, 1979).

> In fact, there is a growing literature which demonstrates that the use of specialty alcohol, other drug abuse, or mental health services tend to decrease the use of general medical services, and, thereby, offsets to some extent the additional costs of the specialty services by reducing costs of general medical services. (*Medical Benefits,* 15 November 1984).

A recent literature review reveals that the evidence for offsets continues to grow (Holder 1987). Several studies will serve to illustrate the returns chemical dependency treatment can make in the area of medical care utilization.

Many comprehensive studies were conducted by a team of researchers who focused on medical claims. In a longitudinal study in California, researchers monitored medical care utilization of families of state employees enrolled in Blue Cross-Blue Shield of California (Holder and Hallan 1978, 1981). Medical care utilization was reviewed for a period prior to coverage for chemical dependency treatment and then monitored for a five-year period. Longitudinal trends from this project are shown in figure 12.3.

Initially, the alcoholics and their families manifested extremely high use rates for medical services, but these dropped sharply after the employees were treated for alcoholism. Although there is some rise in the two- to three-year period after treatment, the rates actually fall below those of the matched control (nonalcoholic) families in the fourth and fifth year after treatment. The study provides evidence for several conclusions: when coverage for alcoholism is available, employees will use the coverage, and when individuals receive treatment, health care utilization appears to be reduced, not only for the alcoholic, but also for family members.

Another Study Confirms Findings

In a larger study, researchers reviewed the claims for federal employees covered by insurance from Aetna Life Insurance Company (Holder et al. 1985). This study compared 1,645 families in which a member was treated for alcoholism with 3,598 families without a claim for treatment. Findings were compatible with the study illustrated by figure 12.3. Prior to treatment, the chemically dependent employee families' medical service costs were twice as high

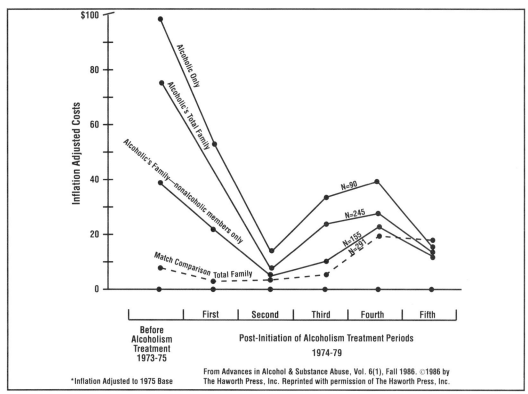

FIGURE 12.3
AVERAGE MONTHLY TOTAL MEDICAL CARE COSTS PER FAMILY - 1973-1979*
BLUE CROSS/BLUE SHIELD OF CALIFORNIA
ENROLLEES FROM STATE EMPLOYEES

as the nonalcoholic families. The medical claims increased over several years and peaked sharply in the six months prior to treatment. After treatment these rates dropped markedly. Based on the longitudinal trends, the researchers estimated that the costs of treatment could be recovered from post-treatment medical cost reductions in approximately three years.

Convergent Validity

Results from scientific studies gain credibility through replication of independent findings by different researchers using different techniques. The term *conver-*

gent validity refers to the convergence of findings from independent sources. Studies conducted by Hazelden Foundation and CATOR (Chemical Abuse Treatment Outcome Registry) yield convergent findings with the studies of claims data.

Results of a Hazelden Study

The Hazelden study involved a random sample of 216 patients treated at programs in Minnesota and North Carolina. The typical patient admitted to these programs was an employed male who had a primary diagnosis of alcoholism and had been drinking for approximately fourteen years. Most of these patients were employed, at least high school graduates, married, and had their treatment funded by insurance.

Data collected at admission covered events during the year prior to treatment. Similar questions were asked after treatment via telephone interviews or mailed questionnaires so that before- and after-treatment comparisons could be made. As seen in figure 12.4, the proportion of patients requiring medical services was substantially reduced in all categories except outpatient medical services. The outpatient rates are lower than the hospitalization rates, suggesting that, since hospitalization is more

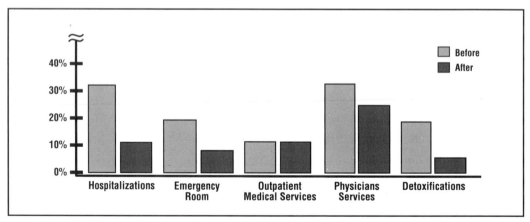

FIGURE 12.4

USE OF HEALTH CARE SERVICES BEFORE AND
AFTER CHEMICAL DEPENDENCY TREATMENT

expensive, the pre-treatment utilization rates for the alcoholics tend to involve relatively expensive services. Furthermore, outpatient medical services often involve treatment of chronic conditions so that marked reductions may not be expected.

Of significance is the fact that, although the pre-treatment rates for this sample are clearly elevated, the hospitalization rates after treatment are near national averages. Approximately 11 percent of the former patients were hospitalized in the year after chemical dependency treatment. This compares favorably with the national statistics that show that 10.3 percent of the adult population being hospitalized at some time during a one-year period (*Medical Benefits*, 31 October 1984).

Confirming Data from CATOR

Results from the CATOR system described in Chapter Ten will serve to replicate and expand the previous findings. The CATOR data draw from treatment populations from 1980 to the present. Thus, repeated findings from CATOR are compatible with the earlier findings. Table 12.1 summarizes some of the pre- and post-treatment medical care utilization rates from CATOR findings analyzed in 1986 and 1988 (Hoffmann and Harrison).

These analyses covered utilization during two years, but the findings are compatible with previously reported one-year outcomes (Hoffmann and Belille 1982; Hoffmann et al. 1984). Consistent findings are that utilization rates are extremely high before treatment, but drop dramatically after treatment. The drop is followed by a rise in use during the second year post-treatment, but nevertheless remains substantially below the pre-treatment rates.

Critics of treatment have suggested two explanations, not related to treatment, for the drop in medical care after treatment. One is a statistical factor known as *regression to the mean*. This occurs when one samples a group that is either abnormally high or low on a measure and then repeats the same measure at a later time. The expectation is that the group will be closer to the general average, or mean, on the second measurement. The critics argue that since some people enter treatment due to a medical crisis, reduced medical use is to be expected at a later time. This

TABLE 12.1
HOSPITAL DAYS UTILIZED

	CATOR 1986 N=1,001			CATOR 1988 N=2,303		
Admission Type	Year Before Treatment	Year 1 After Treatment	Year 2 After Treatment	Year Before Treatment	Year 1 After Treatment	Year 2 After Treatment
Medical	2,462	964	1,214	4,074	2,257	2,676
Psychiatric	749	551	664	1,208	645	1,018
Detox	640	139	288	2,146	548	541

PROPORTION OF PATIENTS HOSPITALIZED

	CATOR 1986 N=1,001			CATOR 1988 N=2,303		
Admission Type	Year Before Treatment	Year 1 After Treatment	Year 2 After Treatment	Year Before Treatment	Year 1 After Treatment	Year 2 After Treatment
Medical	23.5%	11.0%	13.0%	20.6%	10.2%	12.1%
Psychiatric	5.3%	1.9%	2.3%	3.5%	1.2%	1.6%
Detox	7.4%	2.4%	2.2%	10.8%	2.9%	3.5%

would be consistent with the sharp rise in claims just before treatment. The second argument is that medical services offered during treatment might provide some benefit to the patient for the next year and thereby reduce the rate of medical care, independent of any benefit of chemical dependency treatment.

These findings strongly suggest that the key element in the reduction of health care utilization is terminating the use of mood-altering substances.

Recent analyses of the CATOR data challenge these rival hypotheses and suggest that the differences may be largely due to lifestyle changes following treatment, especially abstinence from mood-altering substances. When patients are divided into those who have remained abstinent for two years after treatment versus those who have relapsed, we see substantial differences in total days of hospitalizations (see figure 12.5).

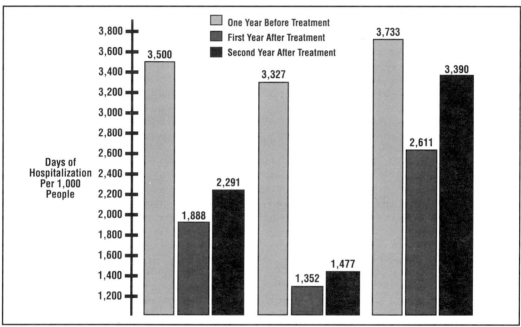

FIGURE 12.5

DAYS OF HOSPITALIZATION BEFORE AND AFTER CHEMICAL DEPENDENCY TREATMENT

When the entire patient population is considered, the drop in hospitalization is approximately 50 percent, but use increases in the second year after treatment. The trends show marked differences, however, when recovering and relapsed patients are analyzed separately.

The relapsed and recovering groups share similarly high hospitalization rates prior to treatment, and both show reductions after treatment. While the number of days of hospitalization for the relapse group drops only modestly in the first year and then rises substantially to near the pre-treatment rate, the hospitalization rate for the recovering patients drops dramatically and remains relatively constant for both years after treatment. These findings strongly suggest that the key element in the reduction of health care utilization is terminating the use of mood-altering substances. Individuals who do return to use appear to show a rebound to high medical care utilization within two years after treatment.

While these findings are important, we suggest some limitations and cautions. The former inpatients who were interviewed at each of four follow-up points over the two-year period are a distinct subset of all patients who entered treatment (Hoffmann and Harrison 1986, 1988). Furthermore, the findings suggest that the demonstrable savings are primarily for those patients who are successful in their abstinence. Thus, one must be very careful in attempting to extrapolate these results to the more general population of all persons receiving treatment. It should also be noted that programs that target people in earlier stages of their chemical dependency may show less dramatic decreases in utilization because their medical complications had not progressed to the same level as others.

Three conclusions seem warranted in view of the evidence.

- First, individuals who abuse alcohol and other drugs tend to place a disproportionate demand on medical service systems.
- Second, successful treatment of chemical dependency reduces these demands for health care, and these reductions are related to abstinence from alcohol and other drugs.
- Third, the magnitude of the post-treatment reductions suggests potential for substantial savings that few other treatments or medical services can match.

EVIDENCE OF COST OFFSETS IN
VOCATIONAL FUNCTIONING AND OTHER LIFE AREAS

Just as substantial returns are seen in medical care utilization, analogous returns can be demonstrated in the area of vocational functioning. As can be seen in figure 12.6, the Hazelden study of a random sample of patients described earlier in this chapter shows significant improvements in reduced absenteeism from work and problems related to poor performance, leading to possible termination. Before treatment, an average of 17 days per year of work was lost due to illness and injury, while after treatment this dropped to an average of 6.5 days per year. National statistics suggest that, on average, workers lose an average of 5 days for illness or injury per year.

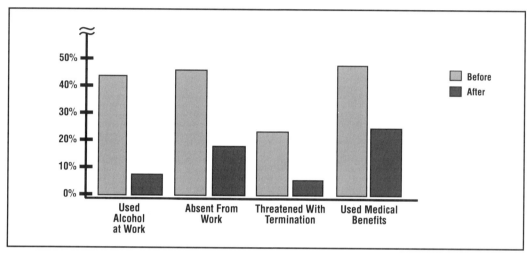

FIGURE 12.6

ALCOHOL AND OTHER DRUG RELATED OCCUPATIONAL PROBLEMS
BEFORE AND AFTER CHEMICAL DEPENDENCY TREATMENT

Table 12.2 presents similar CATOR findings. A substantial proportion of people admitted absenteeism and impaired work performance due to alcohol or other drug use prior to treatment. But after treatment, only a small proportion acknowledged such problems. In fact, frequently, many people who had relapsed did not report work problems. This suggests that there is some positive impact on job attendance and performance, even if treatment is not completely successful in patients achieving abstinence.

Although the areas of medical care utilization and vocational functioning directly affect many payors of chemical dependency treatment, these are by no means the only areas financially affected. The CATOR data also consistently show reductions in arrests and emotional discomfort after treatment. Figure 12.7 from the Hazelden study also illustrates life situations where changes occur after treatment. Arrests

Does Your Program Measure Up?

TABLE 12.2
VOCATIONAL FUNCTIONING BEFORE AND AFTER CHEMICAL DEPENDENCY TREATMENT

	CATOR 1986 N=1,001			CATOR 1988 N=2,303		
	Year Before Treatment	Year 1 After Treatment	Year 2 After Treatment	Year Before Treatment	Year 1 After Treatment	Year 2 After Treatment
Worked full time all year	44.8%	46.5%	49.0%	53.6%	49.2%	53.6%
Absenteeism due to use	30.9%	3.3%	3.5%	39.0%	3.4%	3.7%
Performance Problems	32.4%	2.8%	4.0%	38.7%	2.9%	2.9%
Job Loss	8.0%	0.7%	0.6%	8.4%	1.1%	1.2%

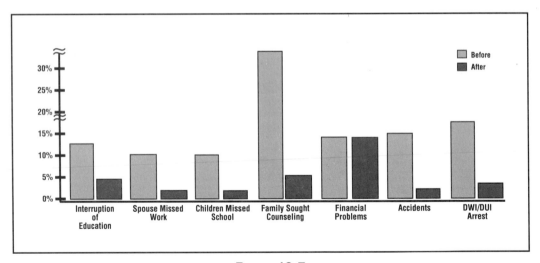

FIGURE 12.7
OTHER PROBLEMS BEFORE AND AFTER CHEMICAL DEPENDENCY TREATMENT

and accidents may be obvious areas affected, but work missed by spouses and missed days of school by children are more subtle changes that take their toll on individuals and ultimately society.

CONCLUSION: THE NEED IS REAL

Many studies demonstrate that alcoholism and other drug abuse are major health and social problems costing society billions of dollars annually through lost productivity, mortality, increased health care costs, accidents, crime, and other problems. In addition, the human suffering is beyond measure. Studies show that chemical dependency treatment is one service that can actually provide substantial returns in terms of financial cost offsets. The question is not whether such returns on the treatment investment exist, but rather how large they are.

Treatment providers can play a role in increasing the proportional return on the investment in treatment. Cost-containment efforts and a continuing focus on cost effectiveness can help improve the efficiency of treatment. In addition, focusing on treatment innovations and improvements to enhance the general outcomes of treatment can also pay dividends in the returns on the treatment investment. In short, continuing efforts to increase treatment efficiency and efficacy will contribute to enhanced cost-offset and cost-benefit advantages for chemical dependency treatment.

REFERENCES

Harwood, H.J. et al. *Economic Costs to Society of Alcohol and Drug Abuse and Mental Illness: 1980.* Research Triangle Park, N.C.: Research Triangle Institute, 1984.

Hoffmann, N.G., and C.A. Belille. *CATOR: Chemical Abuse/Addiction Treatment Outcome Registry, 1982 Report.* St. Paul, Minn: Medical Education and Research Foundation, 1982.

Hoffmann, N.G., J.A. Halikas, and D. Mee-Lee. *The Cleveland Admission, Discharge & Transfer Criteria: A Model for Chemical Dependency Treatment Programs.*

Cleveland, Ohio: Greater Cleveland Hospital Association, 1987.

Hoffmann, N.G., and P.A. Harrison. *CATOR 1986 Report: Findings Two Years After Treatment.* St. Paul, Minn.: Ramsey Clinic, 1986.

Hoffmann, N.G. and P.A. Harrison. *CATOR Report/Treatment Outcome: Adult Inpatients Two Years Later.* St. Paul, Minn.: Ramsey Clinic, 1988.

Hoffmann, N.G., P.A. Harrison, and C.A. Belille. "Multidimensional impact of treatment for substance abuse." *Advances in Alcohol and Substance Abuse* 3 (1984): 83-94.

Holder, H.D. "Alcoholism treatment and potential health care cost savings." *Medical Care* 25 (1987): 52-71.

Holder, H.D., J.O. Blose, and M.J. Gasiorowski. *Alcoholism Treatment Impact on Total Health Care Utilization and Costs: Analysis of the Federal Employee Health Benefit Program with Aetna Life Insurance Company.* Rockville, Md: NIAAA, 1985.

Holder, H.D., and J.B. Hallan. *The California Pilot Program to Provide Health Insurance Coverage for Alcoholism Treatment—One Year After.* Chapel Hill, N.C.: H-2, Inc., 1978.

Holder, H.D., and J.B. Hallan. *Medical Care and Alcoholism Treatment Costs and Utilization: A Five-year Analysis of the California Pilot Project to Provide Health Insurance Coverage for Alcoholism.* Chapel Hill, N.C.: H-2, Inc., 1981.

Holder, H.D. and J.B. Hallan. "Impact of alcoholism treatment on total health care costs: A six-year study." *Advances in Alcohol and Substance Abuse.* 6 (1986): 1-15.

Jones, K.R., and T.R. Vischi. "Impact of alcohol abuse and mental health treatment on medical care utilization: A review of the research literature." *Medical Care* (Supplement) 17 (1979): 1-82.

Levin, H.M. *Cost-Effectiveness: A Primer.* Beverly Hills, Calif.: Sage Press, 1983.

Medical Benefits. Kelly Communications, 410 East Water St., Charlottesville, VA., 15 November 1984 and 31 October 1984.

Saxe, L. et al. *Health Technology Case Study 22: The Effectiveness and Costs of Alcoholism Treatment.*

Washington, D.C.: Office of Technology Assessment, 1983.

Sixth Special Report for the U.S. Congress on Alcohol and Health. Washington, D.C.: U.S. Department of Health and Human Services, 1987.

Spicer, J., T. McKenna, and L. Nyberg. *Apples and Oranges: A Comparison of Inpatient and Outpatient Programs.* Center City, Minn: Hazelden Foundation, 1981.

Warner, K.E., and R.L. Bryan. *Cost-Benefit and Cost-Effectiveness Analysis in Health Care.* Ann Arbor, Mich.: University of Michigan Press, 1982.

Wright, P.C. "How managers should approach alcoholism and drug abuse in the workplace." *Business Quarterly,* Winter 1983.

Thomas McKenna, Ph.D.;
Leslie Tamble; and Jerry Spicer

*At the time of this study, Thomas McKenna
was a candidate for a doctorate in psychology
at the University of Minnesota, and Leslie
Tamble was a staff researcher at Hazelden.*

CHAPTER THIRTEEN

COMPARISON OF HAZELDEN INPATIENT AND OUTPATIENT PROGRAMS

Data for this study were collected by several departments:

- Client background variables were documented in the clients' files by Outpatient Staff.
- Medical Records by entering certain variables on to abstracting forms that were then computer-entered.
- Additional information on all outpatients (104) and on a random sample of 116 inpatients was assembled in order to determine differences in client background and psychological well-being.
- The Quality Assurance department assisted in designing instruments to collect these data. Psychological variables were measured by the Minnesota Multiphasic Personality Inventory (MMPI), which is administered to Hazelden clients within the first week of treatment.
- The Evaluation and Research Department, responsible for the follow-up evaluation process, sent questionnaires to the clients at six and twelve months after discharge. To reach as many of the clients as possible, those not responding to the mailed questionnaire were interviewed by tele-

phone. Questionnaires were also sent to a confirming source for validation of clients' self-report.

CLIENT CHARACTERISTICS

The inpatients and outpatients studied had differing
demographic and socioeconomic characteristics. While
approximately three-fourths of both populations were male,
inpatients were older than outpatients and less likely to be
married. Socioeconomic status of inpatients was somewhat
higher. Perhaps the most pronounced difference between
the two populations was geographical, with almost all outpatients (99 percent) reporting Minnesota residence, while
two-thirds of the inpatients were from out of state.

Equal numbers of inpatients (68 percent) and outpatients (67 percent) reported alcohol-related arrests prior to
admission. Inpatients, however, were more likely to report
previous hospitalizations. Inpatients who have undergone
previous treatments have been found to have a more difficult time maintaining sobriety than those with no prior
treatment (Laundergan 1980).

All patients were examined for the presence of thirty-one
symptoms of alcoholism, using a modification of the
Jellinek symptomatology (Jellinek 1952). These symptoms
included the following indicators of physiological dependence: tremors, morning drinking, loss of control, blackouts, and continuous use for a period exceeding eighteen
hours (Polich et al. 1980). Inpatients were more likely than
outpatients to endorse thirty of the thirty-one symptoms,
and the difference was statistically significant for twenty of
the thirty-one symptoms. Jellinek (1952) arranged the
symptoms in an order that represents increasing severity
of alcoholism. The study showed that inpatients were significantly more likely than outpatients to endorse fifteen of
the last sixteen signs and symptoms, but endorsement
rates did not differ significantly on ten of the first fifteen
symptoms. The data suggest that inpatients endorsed both
a larger number of, and more serious, symptoms than did
outpatients, inferring that inpatients suffered from more
severe alcoholism than did outpatients.

Inpatients were more likely than outpatients to experience changes in their lives as a result of drinking: inpatients were more likely to have

- undergone some kind of treatment,
- lost a job or position,
- tried to escape the effects of their drinking

Somewhat less pronounced is the indication that inpatients were more likely to report decreased tolerance, morning usage, tremors, and continuous usage for a period exceeding eighteen hours.

Diagnostically, patients admitted to treatment are classified as prodromal, crucial, or chronic alcoholics on the basis of the Jellinek (1952) symptomatology. Of the inpatients, 98.3 percent were diagnosed as chronic alcoholics, compared to 85.7 percent of the outpatients.

Measures of quantity of alcohol intake were converted to standard one-ounce units of absolute ethanol. Mean daily intake for inpatients was 21.2 ounces, compared to a mean of 14.6 ounces for outpatients.

Clients were also questioned about their pattern and duration of alcohol use. There was no relationship between pattern of use (continuous, episodic) and treatment location. While duration of alcohol *use* was longer for inpatients, no significant difference was shown in the duration of alcohol *abuse* (defined as time between first intoxication and admission to present treatment).

PSYCHOLOGICAL WELL-BEING

Of 121 outpatients, 104 had completed an MMPI. This group was compared to a random sample of 121 Hazelden inpatients, 116 of whom completed the MMPI. Two-tailed, independent sample t-tests contrasted inpatients and outpatients on MMPI validity, clinical, and special scales.

Inpatient clinical scales showed a generally greater elevation than did outpatient MMPI profiles, suggesting a generally higher level of psychopathology among inpatients. Significant differences were found on Scales 1, 2, and, especially, Scales 7 and 8. Individual scale differences suggest that, in addition to generally greater psychopathology, inpatients reported more somatic complaints (Scale 1), more severe depression (Scale 2), more anxiety (Scale 7), and more bizarre thought and behavior (Scale 8). Inpatients experienced increased levels of subjective distress, depression, and anxiety (Scales 2 and 7), and were more likely to exhibit schizoid and pre-psychotic tendencies (Scales 2, 7 and 8). Interestingly, scores on Scales 4 and 9 were virtually identical, suggesting that the proportion of alcoholics with sociopathic tendencies may be approximately equal in these inpatient and outpatient populations.

Although analyses of two-point and three-point code types were not conducted, evaluations on Scales 2, 7, and 8 suggest that inpatients may be more likely to experience difficulty in establishing warm, rewarding relationships. They are more likely to be introverted and socially withdrawn, lacking social skills, and perceived by others as being cold and aloof. Inpatient elevations on the depression scale (Scale 2) and on Scales 7 and 8, also associated with depression (Hathaway and Meehl 1978), point to a substantially greater frequency of depressive disorders among inpatients.

MMPI special scales were also studied. The Harris-Lingoes subscales indicated that outpatients were more likely to report familial discord than inpatients, but that inpatients were more likely to report social alienation. The latter finding is compatible with the social withdrawal suggested above. Inpatients scored higher than outpatients on the MacAndrew Alcoholism Scale, suggesting the possibility of more severe alcoholism among inpatients.

CLIENT OUTCOMES

Inpatients and outpatients report almost identical outcomes one year after treatment, with inpatients reporting a slightly lower rate of alcohol and other drug use and a higher rate of involvement in AA. Previous research at Hazelden has demonstrated relationships among completing treatment, attending AA, and maintaining a drug-free life. This may be associated with the somewhat lower recovery rate for the outpatients, as fewer outpatients (74 percent) completed treatment compared to the inpatients (85 percent). Outpatients also participated less frequently in AA after treatment. Completing treatment and using AA as a follow-up support system may enable clients to receive more extensive amounts of treatment, which Armor et al. (1978) found to be important in explaining recovery.

CONCLUSIONS

These data support the assertion that a direct comparison between inpatient and outpatient treatment programs is inappropriate. Inpatients exhibited generally greater psychopathology: they reported more somatic complaints, more depression, more anxiety, and more bizarre thoughts and behavior. Inpatient elevations on MMPI Scales 1, 2, and 7 suggest that inpatients were more likely than outpatients to exhibit neurotic tendencies; furthermore, elevations on Scale 8, as well as the 2-7-8 elevation, suggest more schizoid and pre-psychotic tendencies among inpatients. Social alienation and withdrawal seem to characterize a greater proportion of inpatients.

Inpatients scored higher than outpatients on the MacAndrew Alcoholism Scale, were more likely to be diagnosed as chronic alcoholics, and endorsed more of the Jellinek alcoholism symptoms. Inpatients were more likely to endorse such symptoms of physiological dependence as tremors, morning drinking, and continuous use beyond an eighteen-hour period, and inpatients were more likely (47 percent versus 7 percent) to report previous hospitalizations. Inpatients consumed more alcohol than did outpatients. Although inpatients had a longer duration of alcohol use, there were no significant differences in pattern of use or duration of alcohol abuse.

This comparison of inpatient and outpatient client characteristics found that inpatients have more severe alcohol-related problems and symptoms. The major implication of this study is to challenge earlier statements regarding the relative effectiveness of inpatient and outpatient programs (Armor et al. 1978). Although outcomes are similar, client characteristics and program processes are different. Client variables influence outcomes, and comparisons of inpatient and outpatient programs should either control for such variables or employ random assignment of subjects.

Because of differences in client characteristics, the most accurate conclusion may be that the inpatient and outpatient programs are equally effective with their appropriate clients. But we cannot assume that all clients would benefit from either program. Each program has adapted its processes to its client populations and may not be as effective with a different type of client. It is also inappropriate to group short-term hospitalizations with thirty-two-day residential programs or five-session outpatient programs with twenty-session programs. Programs using treatment models that differ in philosophy and intensity should avoid direct comparison of outcomes.

Future research should attend to characteristics of the most successful inpatient and outpatient treatment centers, as well as contrasting successful outpatient centers with successful inpatient centers. The most important treatment characteristic in achieving successful outcomes has yet to be conclusively demonstrated, although amount of treatment is currently the most likely candidate.

Given the limited generalizations of inpatient and outpatient studies, concluding that all inpatient or all outpatient programs should be eliminated is unwarranted. Local comparisons of available inpatient and outpatient programs would, however, seem to be an important part of a cost-effectiveness study. But it is important that such comparisons attend to

- possible heterogeneity within local inpatient and outpatient settings
- heterogeneity of client characteristics between inpatient and outpatient settings
- level of program intensity and peer support

For local communities, the evaluation question may not be "which is more effective, inpatient or outpatient treatment?" but rather, "which of our facilities is most appropriate for treating this type of client with these problems?"

EPILOGUE

Evaluation and research in the field of chemical dependency treatment present not only methodological issues, but conceptual challenges as well. Although treatment has its share of critics and doubters, it is possible for a treatment program to have a reliable and valid outcome evaluation system that meets the program's needs for accountability, quality assurance, and management. And as the case studies indicate, there is evidence from more sophisticated research studies on the overall clinical and cost impact of treatment and rehabilitation programs. The unique concepts of chemical dependency recovery present challenges to the researcher.

Quality of life and spirituality are too often ignored by the research community as "soft" data that cannot be measured. Yet our studies show that these are critical outcomes that must be assessed in our research. Outcome data demonstrate that treatment does work for many people and that recovery is a continuous and variable process as patients and family negotiate their way to sobriety and a better quality of life.

But a scientific perspective requires an understanding that research does not provide immediate proof that treatment works. Over time, further research provides many answers but raises an equal number of new questions. Our efforts today will have unanticipated effects in the future. The purposes of this book have been to summarize what we know and don't know, and to raise our curiosity and increase our commitment to continuing to evaluate and study what we do. In the long run, the benefits accrue to our patients and communities.

My thanks to the authors who have contributed their time and insights and who have made this book a better publication.

— JERRY SPICER

APPENDIX A

CONSULTATION SERVICES

Treatment Outcome/Patient Follow-up

1. *CATOR* —a patient registry and follow-up system
    serving chemical dependency treatment programs.
    For more information, contact

    Norman Hoffmann
    Executive Director
    CATOR
    St. Paul Ramsey Hospital
    640 Jackson St.
    St. Paul, MN 55101
    (612) 221-2740

2. *Hazelden Research Consultation* — provides training
    and consultation services for program development,
    training, evaluation, and quality assurance. For more
    information, contact

    Jerry Spicer
    Chief Operating Officer
    Hazelden Foundation
    P. O. Box 176
    Center City, MN 55012-0176
    (612) 257-4010

    Twin Cities Metropolitan Area: 462-7700

COMPUTER SOFTWARE/INFORMATION SYSTEMS

1. *Computer-Assisted Automated Drinking Evaluation (ADE) and the Substance Abuse/Life Circumstance Evaluation (SALCE)* — the ADE/SALCE is a computer-assisted screening tool that saves time and greatly simplifies the process of screening an individual's use of alcohol and drugs. It is used most extensively in screening DWI/DUI offenders in courts and treatment programs. For more information, contact

   Brian Ellis
   President
   ADE Incorporated
   20 West Washington St.
   Clarkston, MI 48016
   (313) 625-7200

2. *Hazelden BENCHMARKS Management Reporting Software* — BENCHMARKS Management Reporting Software, new from Hazelden, produces six computerized reports: Census, Client Profile, Funding for Treatment, Referent, Service Evaluation, and One-Month Follow-Up reports. BENCHMARKS can be customized to provide reports for inpatient, outpatient, adolescent, and family programs. For more information, contact

   Hazelden Services, Inc.
   1400 Park Ave.
   Minneapolis, MN 55404-1597
   (612) 349-4360

3. *Minnesota Assessment of Chemical Health (MACH —* Questions in this interactive chemical health assessment compare the client's responses to (1) national diagnostic criteria such as the MAST, Mortimer-Filkins, and DSM-III-R, and (2) specific referral/reimbursement criteria such as Blue Cross-Blue Shield, the Foundation for Health Care Evaluation, U.S. Army Tracks, Honeywell EAP, and Minnesota Rule 25. Administration time is under thirty minutes. For more information, contact

James Kincannon
Senior Clinical Psychologist
MACH
Hennepin County Division of Chemical Health
1800 Chicago Ave. S.
Minneapolis, MN 55404
(612) 623-2588

4. *Minnesota Chemical Dependency Adolescent Assessment Project (MCDAAP) Package* — Six years in the making, this clinical assessment package was developed by a consortium of Minnesota chemical dependency service providers and a team of researchers. The battery consists of three primary instruments:

- *Personal Experience Inventory (PEI)* — A multidimensional self-report questionnaire that measures chemical use problem severity, psychosocial risk factors, specialized problem areas, and response distortion tendencies.
- *Adolescent Diagnostic Interview (ADI)* — A structured diagnostic interview primarily organized around DSM-III-R criteria for substance use disorders.
- *Personal Experience Screen Questionnaire (PESQ)* — A brief self-report screening tool that correlates highly with the problem severity scales on the larger questionnaire. For more information contact

Kenneth Winters
Director of Adolescent Health Program
Center for Adolescent Substance Abuse
Box 721, East River Road
University of Minnesota Health Center
Minneapolis, MN 55455

Does Your Program Measure Up?

ACCREDITATION PROGRAMS

1. Commission for the Accreditation of Rehabilitation
   Facilities
   Suite 500, 101 N. Wilmot Rd.,
   Tucson, AZ 85711

2. Joint Commission for the Accreditation of Health Care
   Organizations
   875 N. Michigan Ave.
   Chicago, IL 60611

APPENDIX B
Sample Instruments
ABSTRACTING FORM

1A. FACULTY NUMBER
— — — — — —

1B. HAZELDEN NUMBER
— — — — — —

2. ADMISSION DATE
— — —
Mo. Day Yr.

3. DISCHARGE DATE
— — —
Mo. Day Yr.

4. ADMISSION REFERENT
— —

5. TYPE OF ADMISSION
(01) ___ Voluntary
(02) ___ Other
(09) ___ Unknown

6. PREVIOUS ADMISSIONS
(01) ___ No
(02) ___ Once
(03) ___ Twice
(04) ___ 3 or more
(09) ___ Unknown

7. PREVIOUS PROGRAM
(01) ___ Inpatient
(02) ___ Outpatient
(03) ___ Assessment
(04) ___ Family
(05) ___ Adolescent
(06) ___ Aftercare
(07) ___ Detoxification
(08) ___ Other
(09) ___ None
(99) ___ Unknown

8. PRIMARY PAYMENT
— —

9. RACE
(01) ___ Caucasian
(02) ___ Black
(03) ___ Hispanic
(04) ___ Native American
(05) ___ Asian
(06) ___ Other
(09) ___ Unknown

10. GENDER
(01) ___ Male
(02) ___ Female

11. AGE
— —

12. RELIGION
(01) ___ Protestant
(02) ___ Catholic
(03) ___ Jewish
(04) ___ Agnostic/None
(05) ___ Other
(06) ___ Unknown

13. HOME STATE
— —

14. HOME COUNTY
— —

15. MARITAL STATUS
(01) ___ Single
(02) ___ Married
(03) ___ Widowed
(04) ___ Separated
(05) ___ Divorced
(06) ___ Living Together
(09) ___ Unknown

16. OCCUPATION
— —

17. EDUCATION
(01) ___ Elementary Grades
(02) ___ High School (Incomplete)
(03) ___ High School Graduate or GED
(04) ___ College (Incomplete)
(05) ___ A.A. Degree
(06) ___ College Graduate
(07) ___ Advanced Degree
(08) ___ Voc. Training
(09) ___ Unknown

18. AGE OF FIRST USE
— —

19. AGE OF FIRST PROBLEMS
— —

20. AGE OTHERS BEGAN TO COMPLAIN
— —

21. RELATED ARRESTS
— —

22. DWI ARRESTS
— —

23. PREVIOUS TREATMENT
— —

24. A.A. PARTICIPATION   (01) ___ Yes (02) ___ No (09) ___ Unknown

CHEMICAL USE
(25) ___ Alcohol
(26) ___ Sedatives
(27) ___ Stimulants
(28) ___ Hallucinogens
(29) ___ Opiates
(30) ___ Cannabis
(31) ___ Inhalants
(32) ___ Cocaine
(33) ___ Other

(34) ___ ___ **CHEMICAL OF CHOICE**
(35) ___ ___ **PROBLEM CHEMICAL**
(36) ___ ___ **NO. DETOX HOURS**
(37) ___ ___ **NO. REHAB DAYS**

(38) FAMILY PROGRAM INVOLVEMENT
(01) ___ Yes
(02) ___ No
(03) ___ Unknown

(39) DISCHARGE STATUS
— —

(40) AFTERCARE REFERRALS
(01) ___ A.A.
(02) ___ Aftercare
(03) ___ Outpatient
(04) ___ E.A.P. Service
(05) ___ Halfway House
(06) ___ _____
(07) ___ _____
(08) ___ _____
(09) ___ Other
(10) ___ None
(99) ___ Unknown

(41) YEARLY FAMILY INCOME
_____

194

Does Your Program Measure Up?

Service Evaluation Questionnaire

This questionnaire is part of our follow-up services. This information will be used by _____ to evaluate and improve services. Please check the most appropriate response per question unless otherwise instructed. Your responses will be confidential. Thank you for your help.

| **CONFIDENTIAL** |
| Number: _____ |
| _____ |

1. During the year **prior** to your admission, which chemical dependency services or programs did you use? (*Please check all that apply.*)

_____ (01) Residential free-standing chemical dependency treatment
_____ (02) Hospital-based inpatient chemical dependency treatment
_____ (03) Outpatient chemical dependency treatment
_____ (04) Detoxification
_____ (05) Halfway house
_____ (06) Chemical dependency assessment
_____ (07) Went to Alcoholics Anonymous/ Narcotics Anonymous
_____ (08) Inpatient psychiatric treatment
_____ (09) Mental health counseling services
_____ (10) Other: _____

2. Have you ever been admitted to _____ for chemical dependency treatment before?
_____ (01) No
_____ (02) Yes, once
_____ (03) Yes, twice
_____ (04) Yes, three times or more

3. If you have been admitted to _____ for treatment before, which program(s) did you enter? (*Check all that apply.*)

_____ (01) No previous admission
_____ (02) Inpatient
_____ (03) Outpatient
_____ (04) Adolescent
_____ (05) Family program
_____ (06) Aftercare program
_____ (07) Assessment program
_____ (08) Detoxification
_____ (09) Other
_____ (10) Custom slot 1 _____
_____ (11) Custom slot 2 _____
_____ (12) Custom slot 3 _____

4. Which of these describes your present marital situation?

_____ (01) Single
_____ (02) Married
_____ (03) Widowed
_____ (04) Separated
_____ (05) Divorced
_____ (06) Living together

5. What is your present employment status?

_____ (01) Full-time job
_____ (02) Self-employed
_____ (03) Part-time job
_____ (04) Homemaker
_____ (05) Student
_____ (06) Retired
_____ (07) Military
_____ (08) Unemployed

Copyright © Hazelden Foundation, 1990. All rights reserved.

GP-5/90

6. What was your usual occupation before admission? _____

7. Which of these best describes your highest education level? (*Check only one.*)

_____ (01) Elementary grades   _____ (05) Associate Arts Degree
_____ (02) High school (incomplete)   _____ (06) College graduate
_____ (03) High school graduate or GED   _____ (07) Advanced degree
_____ (04) College (incomplete)   _____ (08) Vocational training

8. Which of these categories best represents your yearly family income?

_____ (01) Less than 20,000   _____ (04) $40,000 to $49,999
_____ (02) $20,00 to $29,999   _____ (05) $50,000 and above
_____ (03) $30,000 to $39,999   _____ (06) Prefer not to answer
                                         _____ (07) Don't know

9. What was the primary source of payment for your treatment? (*Check one only.*)

_____ (01) Self payment   _____ (07) Medicaid
_____ (02) Family   _____ (08) Custom slot 1 _____
_____ (03) Commercial Insurance   _____ (09) Custom slot 2 _____
_____ (04) BC/BS   _____ (10) Custom slot 3 _____
_____ (05) HMO   _____ (11) Other
_____ (06) Medicare   _____ (99) Unknown

REFERRAL INFORMATION

---

10. How did you hear about the _____ treatment program?

_____ (01) Former patient   _____ (08) Phone book
_____ (02) Physician   _____ (09) Newspaper ads
_____ (03) Psychologist/counselor   _____ (10) Custom slot 1 _____
_____ (04) Parents   _____ (11) Custom slot 2 _____
_____ (05) School counselor   _____ (12) Custom slot 2 _____
_____ (06) Radio Ads   _____ (13) Other
_____ (07) TV Ads

11. How was it decided that you should receive treatment? (*Please check all that describe how the referral was made.*)

_____ (01) I decided I needed treatment   _____ (09) A psychologist/counselor
_____ (02) My supervisor at work told me I had   recommended it
           to go   _____ (10) Another treatment center
_____ (03) My company's counselor suggested it   recommended it
_____ (04) A co-worker suggested it   _____ (11) I was referred through the intervention
_____ (05) A friend suggested it   process
_____ (06) A family member suggested it   _____ (12) My attorney recommended it
_____ (07) A former patient suggested it   _____ (13) Court ordered
_____ (08) A physician recommended it   _____ (14) Other: _____

               GP-5/90

Does Your Program Measure Up?

12. At the time you came to treatment, did your company have an employee assistance program?

_____ (1) Yes, they referred me to _____
_____ (2) Yes, but they did not refer me to _____
_____ (3) No, they don't have an employee assistance program
_____ (4) Don't know
_____ (5) Not applicable

OTHER AREAS

The following is a list of areas of your life. Choose the response which best describes your status in each of these areas before treatment. (*Be sure to answer each item.*)

	(01) Excellent	(02) Good	(03) Fair	(04) Poor	(05) Not Applicable
13. Relationship with spouse/significant other	_____	_____	_____	_____	_____
14. Relationships with immediate family	_____	_____	_____	_____	_____
15. Relationships with friends	_____	_____	_____	_____	_____
16. Relationship with Higher Power	_____	_____	_____	_____	_____
17. Self-image (how you feel about yourself)	_____	_____	_____	_____	_____
18. Physical health	_____	_____	_____	_____	_____
19. Ability to handle problems	_____	_____	_____	_____	_____
20. Job/school performance	_____	_____	_____	_____	_____
21. Overall quality of life	_____	_____	_____	_____	_____

PATIENT EVALUATION

Please check "agree" if you agree with the statement or "disagree" if you disagree with the statement most of the time.

	(01) Agree	(02) Disagree
22. Counselors had very little time for patients	_____	_____
23. Counselors didn't explain what treatment was all about	_____	_____
24. Patients felt prepared to begin a new lifestyle after treatment	_____	_____
25. Staff were sincerely interested in each patient	_____	_____
26. Unit expectations were clearly understood by all patients	_____	_____
27. Things were sometimes very disorganized around here	_____	_____
28. Staff told patients when they were making progress	_____	_____
29. I felt I had the right to disagree with staff and to voice my opinion	_____	_____
30. Patients here rarely become upset about the treatment process	_____	_____
31. There was unauthorized use of mood-altering chemicals in the unit that the staff was unaware of	_____	_____

SERVICE EVALUATION

Looking back over your participation in this program, how satisfied were you with these aspects of the program? (*Be sure to answer each item.*)

	(01) Very Satisfied	(02) Mostly Satisfied	(03) Indifferent or Mildly Dissatisfied	(04) Quite Dissatisfied	(05) Does Not Apply
32. Admission procedures	___	___	___	___	___
33. Detoxification procedures	___	___	___	___	___
34. Orientation to treatment program	___	___	___	___	___
35. Medical/nursing staff	___	___	___	___	___
36. Your treatment plan	___	___	___	___	___
37. Meals	___	___	___	___	___
38. Procedures for visiting	___	___	___	___	___
39. Telephone	___	___	___	___	___
40. Bookstore/Gift Shop	___	___	___	___	___
41. Housekeeping	___	___	___	___	___
42. Recreation/leisure time	___	___	___	___	___
43. Building and grounds	___	___	___	___	___
44. A.A. orientation	___	___	___	___	___
45. Aftercare planning	___	___	___	___	___
46. Discharge procedures	___	___	___	___	___
47. Custom Slot 1 _____	___	___	___	___	___
48. Custom Slot 2 _____	___	___	___	___	___
49. Custom Slot 3 _____	___	___	___	___	___

Comments regarding these aspects: _____

GP-5/90

Does Your Program Measure Up?

Please rate these aspects of the program in terms of how helpful they were to you: (*Be sure to answer each item.*)

	(01) Much Help	(02) Some Help	(03) Little Help	(04) No Help	(05) Does Not Apply
50. Readings/homework assignments	_____	_____	_____	_____	_____
51. Working the 4th and 5th Steps	_____	_____	_____	_____	_____
52. Time alone for thought	_____	_____	_____	_____	_____
53. Informal conversations with other patients	_____	_____	_____	_____	_____
54. Individual counseling sessions	_____	_____	_____	_____	_____
55. Group therapy	_____	_____	_____	_____	_____
56. Family sessions	_____	_____	_____	_____	_____
57. Lectures/chemical dependency education	_____	_____	_____	_____	_____
58. Films	_____	_____	_____	_____	_____
59. Health education	_____	_____	_____	_____	_____
60. Spiritual guidance	_____	_____	_____	_____	_____
61. Employment/educational guidance	_____	_____	_____	_____	_____
62. Legal assistance	_____	_____	_____	_____	_____
63. Relaxation training	_____	_____	_____	_____	_____
64. Custom Slot 1 _____ . . .	_____	_____	_____	_____	_____
65. Custom Slot 2 _____ . . .	_____	_____	_____	_____	_____
66. Custom Slot 3 _____ . . .	_____	_____	_____	_____	_____

67. Overall, how satisfied were you with the services you received?

_____ (01) Very satisfied
_____ (02) Mostly satisfied
_____ (03) Indifferent or mildly dissatisfied
_____ (04) Quite dissatisfied-please explain _____

_____

_____

_____

68. Of all the lectures you heard, which was the best? Why? _____

_____

_____

_____

GP-5/90

69. Was interaction with other patients helpful?

   _____ (01) Yes, very helpful
   _____ (02) Yes, somewhat helpful
   _____ (03) Not very helpful
   _____ (04) Not helpful at all-please explain: _____

   _____

   _____

70. Was interaction with counselors/staff helpful?

   _____ (01) Yes, very helpful
   _____ (02) Yes, somewhat helpful
   _____ (03) Not very helpful
   _____ (04) Not helpful at all-please explain: _____

   _____

   _____

71. Do you feel you were treated with dignity and respect by _____

   _____ (01) Yes
   _____ (02) No

72. Do you feel your length of your stay at _____ was:

   _____ (01) Too short?
   _____ (02) About right?
   _____ (03) Too long?
   _____ (04) Not helpful at all — please explain: _____

   _____

   _____

73. Did you feel adequately informed about your condition, treatment, and what happens after discharge?

   _____ (01) Yes
   _____ (02) No — please explain: _____

   _____

   _____

74. Do you have any further suggestions? _____

   _____

   _____

THANK YOU

Does Your Program Measure Up?

Twelve-Month Follow-Up Questionnaire

As part of our follow-up services, this one-year questionnaire is designed to help you evaluate your progress and to indicate in what ways you might need some assistance. This information will be used to evaluate and improve program services. Please check the most appropriate response or fill in the answer. Choose *only one* response per question unless otherwise instructed. Your responses will be confidential. Thank you for your help.

CONFIDENTIAL
Number: _____
_____

ALCOHOL AND DRUG USE QUANTITY

1. Which statement best describes your use of **alcohol** compared to what it was before treatment? (*Check one*)

    _____ (01) I have not used any alcohol
    _____ (02) I use alcohol, but not as much
    _____ (03) I use about as much
    _____ (04) I use more

2. Which statement best describes your use of **drugs**, other than alcohol, compared to what it was before treatment? (*Check one*)

    _____ (01) I have not used any drugs
    _____ (02) I have used drugs, but only for medical reasons
    _____ (03) I use drugs, but not as much
    _____ (04) I use about as much
    _____ (05) I use more

If you have not used alcohol or drugs, skip to question 6.

3. If you have used alcohol or other drugs since treatment, which best describes why? (*Check one*)

    _____ (01) Craving
    _____ (02) Impulsive action, spur-of-the-moment decision
    _____ (03) Social/peer pressure
    _____ (04) Anxious, nervous mood
    _____ (05) Depressed mood
    _____ (06) Tense or difficult situation
    _____ (07) Happy or exciting situation
    _____ (08) Thought the risks were minimal
    _____ (09) Other: _____

4. If you have used alcohol or other drugs since treatment, how would you describe your use? (*Check one*)

    _____ (01) I've used for a period of time, then stopped, and have remained abstinent
    _____ (02) I've had 2 or more periods of use with periods of abstinence
    _____ (03) Since I started, I've used more or less continuously

5. If you have used alcohol or other drugs since treatment, has your use caused you any problems? (*Check one*)

    _____ (01) Yes, and I quit
    _____ (02) Yes, but I continue to use
    _____ (03) No, no problems

TYPES OF SUPPORT SINCE PROGRAM PARTICIPATION
---

6. Have you used any of these services for alcohol or other drug problems since treatment? Please check each item.

Yes No
___ ___ (01) Residential free-standing chemical dependency treatment
___ ___ (02) Hospital-based inpatient chemical dependency treatment
___ ___ (03) Outpatient treatment
___ ___ (04) Detoxification
___ ___ (05) Went to Alcoholics Anonymous
___ ___ (06) Inpatient psychiatric treatment
___ ___ (07) Mental health counseling services
___ ___ (08) Halfway house
___ ___ (09) Chemical dependency assessment
___ ___ (10) Private counseling
___ ___ (11) Group therapy
___ ___ (12) Employer provided counseling (EAP)
___ ___ (13) Aftercare
___ ___ (14) Physician
___ ___ (15) Other: _____

A.A./N.A. PARTICIPATION AND SPIRITUALITY
---

7. How frequently are you attending A.A./N.A. meetings? (*Check one*)

_____ (01) More than once a week   _____ (04) About once a month
_____ (02) About once a week   _____ (05) Less than once a month
_____ (03) 2 or 3 times a month   _____ (06) I am not attending

Have you participated in the following A.A. activities since treatment?

	(01) Yes	(02) No	(03) Not Sure
8. Have you done 12th Step work?	_____	_____	_____
9. Have you sponsored an A.A./N.A. member?	_____	_____	_____
10. Do you have an A.A./N.A. sponsor?	_____	_____	_____
11. Has your spouse or significant other ever attended Al-Anon since your treatment?	_____	_____	_____
12. Are you involved in any support groups?	_____	_____	_____

13. Whom do you talk with most often? (*Check one*)

_____ (01) No one   _____ (06) A.A./N.A. sponsor or contact
_____ (02) Spouse/significant other   _____ (07) Clergy
_____ (03) Parents   _____ (08) Counselor
_____ (04) Children   _____ (09) Other: _____
_____ (05) Friend

GP-5/90

Does Your Program Measure Up?

14. Did your treatment have anything to do with acquiring or strengthening this relationship?

___ Yes
___ No

15. How frequently do you maintain contact with a Higher Power through prayer and meditation?

_____ (01) Less often
_____ (02) More often

16. What is your present employment status? (*Check one*)

_____ (01) Full-time job   _____ (05) Student
_____ (02) Self-employed   _____ (06) Retired
_____ (03) Part-time job   _____ (07) Military
_____ (04) Homemaker   _____ (08) Unemployed

17. Does this represent a change since treatment?

_____ (01) Yes, change for the better
_____ (02) Yes, change for the worse
_____ (03) No change

EMPLOYMENT

---

18. How long have you worked at your present job? (*Check one*)

_____ (01) 0 to 5 months   _____ (04) More than 3 years
_____ (02) 6 to 11 months   _____ (05) Does not apply
_____ (03) 1 to 3 years

Compared to the year before your treatment, how often have the following occurred?

	(1) More Often	(2) About as Often	(3) Less Often	(4) Never Occurred	(5) Does Not Apply
19. Using sick days/medical leave	_____	_____	_____	_____	_____
20. Having unexcused absences	_____	_____	_____	_____	_____
21. Using Worker's Compensation	_____	_____	_____	_____	_____
22. Fired because of chemical use	_____	_____	_____	_____	_____
23. Having accidents on the job	_____	_____	_____	_____	_____
24. Problems at work because of chemical use	_____	_____	_____	_____	_____

GP-5/90

Since treatment, how have the following changed? (*Check one*)

	(01) Much Improved	(02) Somewhat Improved	(03) Same	(04) Somewhat Worse	(05) Much Worse	(06) Does Not Apply
25. Attendance on the job	_____	_____	_____	_____	_____	_____
26. Attitude on the job	_____	_____	_____	_____	_____	_____
27. Performance on the job	_____	_____	_____	_____	_____	_____
28. Overall job satisfaction	_____	_____	_____	_____	_____	_____

LEGAL

29. Have you been arrested in the year since treatment?

_____ Yes
_____ No

If you answered ''no'' to above question, skip to question 35

Compared to the year before your treatment, how often have the following occurred?

	(01) More Often	(02) About as Often	(03) Less Often	(04) Never Occurred	(05) Does Not Apply
30. Arrested for driving while intoxicated	_____	_____	_____	_____	_____
31. Arrested for a crime committed while intoxicated	_____	_____	_____	_____	_____
32. Arrested for possession	_____	_____	_____	_____	_____
33. Arrested for any other offense	_____	_____	_____	_____	_____
34. Spent time in jail	_____	_____	_____	_____	_____

HEALTH CARE

Compared to the year before your treatment, how often have the following occurred?

	(01) More Often	(02) About as Often	(03) Less Often	(04) Never Occurred	(05) Does Not Apply
35. Spent time in the hospital because of chemical use	_____	_____	_____	_____	_____
36. Spent time in the hospital for other reasons.	_____	_____	_____	_____	_____
37. Used emergency room services	_____	_____	_____	_____	_____
38. Visited a physician.	_____	_____	_____	_____	_____
39. Sought counseling services	_____	_____	_____	_____	_____

Does Your Program Measure Up?

ALCOHOL AND OTHER DRUG USE FREQUENCY

Which of the following best describes your frequency of use in the last month?

	(01) No use	(02) Less than once a month	(03) 1-3 times per month	(04) Weekly (1-2 days a week)	(05) 3-5 days a week	(06) Daily
40. Alcohol	____	____	____	____	____	____
41. Sedatives	____	____	____	____	____	____
42. Stimulants	____	____	____	____	____	____
43. Hallucinogens	____	____	____	____	____	____
44. Opiates	____	____	____	____	____	____
45. Marijuana & hashish	____	____	____	____	____	____
46. Inhalants	____	____	____	____	____	____
47. Cocaine or ''crack''.	____	____	____	____	____	____
48. Other	____	____	____	____	____	____

SOCIAL

49. Which of these describes your present marital status?

____ (01) Single   ____ (04) Separated

____ (02) Married   ____ (05) Divorced

____ (03) Widowed   ____ (06) Living together

50. Does this marital status represent a change since program participation?

____ (01) Yes, a change for the better

____ (02) Yes, a change for the worse

____ (03) No change

QUALITY OF LIFE

The following is a list of life areas. For each area, choose the response that best describes how you have changed compared to before treatment.

	(01) Much Improved	(02) Somewhat Improved	(03) Same	(04) Somewhat Worse	(05) Much Worse	(06) Does Not Apply
51. Relationship with spouse/ significant other	____	____	____	____	____	____
52. Relationships with immediate family	____	____	____	____	____	____
53. Relationships with friends . .	____	____	____	____	____	____
54. Relationship with Higher Power	____	____	____	____	____	____

	(01) Much Improved	(02) Somewhat Improved	(03) Same	(04) Somewhat Worse	(05) Much Worse	(06) Does Not Apply
55. Self-image (how you feel about yourself)	_____	_____	_____	_____	_____	_____
56. Emotional health	_____	_____	_____	_____	_____	_____
57. Physical health	_____	_____	_____	_____	_____	_____
58. Ability to handle problems . .	_____	_____	_____	_____	_____	_____
59. Job/school performance	_____	_____	_____	_____	_____	_____
60. Overall quality of life	_____	_____	_____	_____	_____	_____

SUMMARY

61. Overall, how satisfied are you with the services you received?

_____ (01) Very satisfied

_____ (02) Mostly satisfied

_____ (03) Indifferent or mildly dissatisfied

_____ (04) Quite dissatisfied — please explain: _____

_____

62. Do you have any other comments for us?

_____

_____

_____

63. Is there any way that we can be of assistance to you? If so, please write your correct address and telephone number below.

_____

_____

_____

My new address is:

_____
Name

_____
Address

_____
City   State   Zip

_____
Telephone Number

THANK YOU!

BIBLIOGRAPHY

COST BENEFIT STUDIES

Aldrete, J.S., H. Jiminez, and N.B. Halpern. "Evaluation and treatment of acute and chronic pancreatitis: A review of 380 cases." *Annals of Surgery* 191 (1980): 664-71.

Ashley, M.H., et al. "The physical disease characteristics of inpatient alcoholics." *Journal of Studies on Alcohol* 42 (1981): 1-15.

Barchha, R., M. Stewart, and S. Guze. "The prevalence of alcoholism among general hospital ward patients." *American Journal of Psychiatry* 125 (1968): 681-84.

Cahalan, D. *Problem Drinkers*. San Francisco: Jossey-Bass, 1976.

Craig, J.R. et al. "An autopsy survey of clinical and anatomic diagnoses associated with alcoholism." *Archives of Pathology and Laboratory Medicine* 104 (1980): 452-55.

Fourth Special Report to the U.S. Congress on Alcohol and Health. Rockville, Md.: National Institute of Alcohol Abuse on Alcoholism, 1981.

Harwood, H.J. et al. *Economic Costs to Society of Alcohol and Drug Abuse and Mental Illness: 1980*. Research Triangle Park, N.C.: Research Triangle Institute, 1984.

Hoffmann, N.G., and C.A. Belille. *CATOR: Chemical Abuse/Addiction Treatment Outcome Registry, 1982 report*. St. Paul, Minn.: St. Paul Medical Education and Research Foundation.

Holder, H.D., and J.B. Hallan. *Medical Care and Alcoholism Treatment Costs and Utilization: A Five Year Analysis of the California Pilot Project to Provide Health Insurance Coverage for Alcoholism*. Washington, D.C.: NIAAA. December 1981.

Jackson-Beeck, M. "Cost-effective chemical dependency treatment." Interstudy, Minneapolis, Minn., 1984.

Kolb, D., and E.K.E. Gunderson. "Medical histories of problem drinkers during their first twelve years of naval service." *Journal of Studies on Alcohol* 44 (1983): 84-94.

Levin, H.M. *Cost-Effectiveness: A Primer.* Beverly Hills, Calif.: Sage Publications, 1983.

McCusker, J., C. Cherubin, and S. Zimberg. "Prevalence of alcoholism in general municipal hospital population." *New York State Journal of Medicine* 71 (1976): 751-54.

Moore, R.A. "The prevalence of alcoholism in a community general hospital." *American Journal of Psychiatry* 128 (1971): 1277-81.

National Institute of Alcohol Abuse on Alcoholism, The Office of Personnel Management and Aetna. *The Alcoholism Report* 12 (1) (28 March 1984).

Saxe, L. et al. *Health Technology Case Study 22: The Effectiveness and Costs of Alcoholism Treatment.* Washington, D.C.: Office of Technology Assessment, March 1983.

Schmidt, W., and R.E. Popham. "Sex differences in mortality: A comparison of male and female alcoholics." Ed. O.J. Kalant. In *Research Advances in Alcohol and Drug Problems.* Vol. 5. New York: Plenum Press, 1980.

Schramm, C.J. "Evaluating industrial alcoholism programs: A human capital approach." *Journal of Studies on Alcohol.* 41 (1980): 702-13.

Soloman, J. et al. "Emergency-room physicians' recognition of alcohol misuse." *Journal of Studies on Alcohol* 41 (1980): 702-13.

U.S. Department of Health and Human Services. *Alcoholism Treatment Programs Within Prepaid Group Practice HMO's: A Final Report.* Washington, D.C.: NIAAA. May, 1982.

U.S. Department of Health and Human Services. *Development of Cost Simulation Study of Alcoholism Insurance Packages.* Executive Summary. Washington, D.C.: NIAAA, May 1983.

Warner, K.E., and R.L. Bryan. *Cost-Benefit and Cost-Effectiveness Analysis in Health Care.* Ann Arbor, Mich.: University of Michigan Press, 1982.

Wright, P.C. "How managers should approach alcoholism and drug abuse in the work place." *Business Quarterly* (Winter 1983).

DATA ANALYSIS AND RESEARCH METHODS

Interviewer's Manual. Ann Arbor, Mich.: Institute for Social Research, University of Michigan, 1976.

Klecka, William R., Norman H. Nie, and C. Hadlai. *Statistical Package for the Social Sciences Primer.* New York: McGraw-Hill, 1975.

Rutman, Leonard, ed. *Evaluation Research Methods: A Basic Guide.* Beverly Hills, Calif.: Sage Publications, 1977.

Selltiz, Claire, Lawrence S. Wrightshan, and Stuart W. Cook. *Research Methods in Social Relations.* New York: Holt, Rinehart and Winston, 1976.

Williamson, John B., David A. Karp, and Dalphine P. Karp. *The Research Craft: An Introduction to Social Science Methods.* New York: Little, Brown, 1977.

EVALUATION

Anderson, D.J., S.M.L. Kammeier, and H.L. Holmes. *Applied Research: Impact on Decision Making.* Center City, Minn.: Hazelden Educational Materials, 1978.

Attkisson, C. Clifford et al. *Evaluation of Human Services Programs.* New York: Academic Press, 1978.

Baekland, Frederick, Lawrence Lundwall, and Benjamin Kissin. "Methods for the treatment of Chronic Alcoholism: A critical appraisal." In *Research Advances in Alcohol and Drug Problems: Volume II.* New York: John Wiley and Sons, 1975.

Brissett, Dennis D. *Delayed Pathways to Recovery.* Hazelden Research Notes, No. 3, February, 1978. Center City, Minn.: Hazelden Foundation.

Davis, Howard R., and Susan E. Salasin. "The utilization of evaluation," *Handbook of Evaluation Research: Volume I.* Beverly Hills, Calif.: Sage Publications, 1975.

Ellwood, Paul M. et al. *Assuring the Quality of Health Care.* Minneapolis: InterStudy, 1973.

Kay, Isabel et al. *The Problem Oriented Health Record.* Hamilton, Ontario: McMaster University Medical Centre, 1973.

Kiresuk, Thomas J., and Robert E. Sherman. "Goal attainment scaling: A general method for evaluating comprehensive community mental health programs." *Community Mental Health Journal* 4 (6) (1968): 443-53.

Kruse, Gregory et al. *A Manual on the Basics of Alcohol-Related Program Evaluation.*

Milcarek, Barry I., and Elmer Struening. "Evaluation methodology: A selective bibliography." *Handbook of Evaluation Research: Volume I.* Beverly Hills, Calif.: Sage Publications, 1975.

Patton, Michael Quinn. *Utilization-Focused Evaluation.* Beverly Hills, Calif.: Sage Publications, 1978.

Patton, Michael Quinn. *Qualitative Evaluation.* Beverly Hills, Calif.: Sage Publications, 1980.

Quick Evaluation Methodology. Executive Office of the President: Special Action Office for Drug Abuse Prevention, 1973.

Rutman, Leonard, and Dick Delong. *Federal Level Evaluation.* Ottawa, Ontario: Carleton University Graphic Services, 1976.

Salasin, Susan. "Exploring goal-free evaluation: An Interview with Michael Scriven." *Evaluation* 2 (1) (1974): 9-16.

Schulberg, Herbert C., and Jeanette M. Jerrell, eds. *The Evaluator and Management.* Beverly Hills, Calif.: Sage Publications, 1979.

Smart, Reginald G. "Trapped administrators: An evaluation of social and community development programs." *Addictions* 19 (4) (1972): 46-57.

Suchman, Edward A. *Evaluation Research: Principles and Practice in Public Service and Social Action Programs.* New York: Russell Sage Foundation, 1967.

Wolfensberger, Wolf, and Linda Glenn. *Program Analysis of Service Systems: Field Manual.* Toronto: Spaling Printing Company, 1974.

FOLLOW-UP AND OUTCOME

Armor, David J., Michael J. Polich, and Harriet B. Stambul. *Alcoholism and Treatment.* Santa Monica, Calif.: The Rand Corporation, 1976.

Davies, D.L., Michael Shepherd, and Edgar Myers. "The two-year's prognosis of 50 alcohol addicts after treatment in hospital." *Quarterly Journal of Studies on Alcohol* 17 (1956): 485-502.

Eagleston, J. and A. Mothershead. "Data collection instructions and procedures." *Alcoholism Program Monitoring System Procedures Manual.* Vol. 1. Metro Park, Calif.: Stanford Research Institute, 1975.

Emrick, Chad D. "A review of psychologically oriented treatment of alcoholism." *Quarterly Journal of Studies on Alcoholism.* 35 (1974): 523-49.

Laundergan, J.C. *Easy Does It! Alcoholism Treatment Outcomes, Hazelden and the Minnesota Model.* Center City, Minn.: Hazelden Educational Materials, 1982.

Laundergan, J.C., and Mary Leo Kammeier. *The Outcome of Treatment: Patients Admitted to Hazelden in 1975.* Center City, Minn.: Hazelden Educational Materials, 1977.

Miller, William R., V. Lloyd Crawford, and Cheryl A. Taylor. "Significant others as corroborative sources for problem drinkers." *Addictive Behaviors.* 4 (1979): 67-70.

Moos, Rudolf, and Fredric Bliss. "Difficulty of follow-up and outcomes of alcoholism treatment." *Journal of Studies on Alcoholism* 39 (3) (1978): 473-90.

Pattison, E.M. et al. "Abstinence and normal drinking: An assessment of changes in drinking patterns in alcoholics after treatment." *Quarterly Journal of Studies on Alcohol* 29 (1968): 610-33.

Patton, Michael Quinn. *Validity and Reliability of Hazelden Treatment Follow-up Data.* Center City: Hazelden Educational Materials, 1978.

Patton, Michael Quinn. *The Outcomes of Treatment: A Study of Patients Admitted to Hazelden in 1976.* Center City, Minn.: Hazelden Foundation, 1979.

Pickens, Roy et al. "Relapse by alcohol abusers." *Alcoholism: Clinical and Experimental Research* 9 (1985): 244-47.

Pittman, David J., and Robert L. Tate. "A comparison of two treatment programs for alcoholics." *Quarterly Journal of Studies on Alcohol* 30 (1969): 889-99.

QUESTIONNAIRE DEVELOPMENT

Berdie, Doug, John Anderson, and Marsha Niebuhr. *Questionnaires: Design and Use.* Metuchen, N.J.: Scarecrow Press, 1986.

Ralph G. Connor Alcohol Research Reference Files (CARRF). Piscataway, N.J.: Center of Alcohol Studies, Rutgers University.

Dillman, Don A. *Mail and Telephone Surveys: The Total Design Method.* New York: John Wiley and Sons, Inc. 1978.

Groves, Robert M., and Robert L. Kahn. *Surveys by Telephone: A National Comparison With Personal Interviews.* New York: Academic Press, 1979.

Kiresuk, Thomas J. *Organizational Readiness to Accept Program Evaluation Questionnaire.* Minneapolis: Minneapolis Medical Research Foundation, 1976.

Nehemkis, Alexis, Mary A. Macarie, and Dan J. Lehieri, eds. *Research Issues 12: Drug Abuse Instrument Handbook.* Washington, D.C.: U.S. Government Printing Office, 1976.

GENERAL

Webster's Ninth New Collegiate Dictionary. Springfield, Mass.: Merriam-Webster, 1985.

INDEX

A

Absenteeism, 174-177

Abstinence:
  CATOR monitored programs, 121-122
  Minnesota Model programs, 104-108

Adolescent treatment, 135-137
  Chemical Abuse Treatment Registry (CATOR), 142-144
  compared with adult treatment, 146-147
  conclusions about, 145-146
  Drug Abuse Reporting Program (DARP), 137-138
  future research considerations, 149-152
  health care trends, 147-149
  Pennsylvania Substance-Abuse System (UDCS), 140-142
  smaller studies, 144-145
  Treatment Outcome Prospective Study (TOPS), 138-140

Aetna Life Insurance Company, 168-169

Aftercare issues, 67

Alcoholics Anonymous, philosophy of, 10

Alcoholics Anonymous model, 4-6

Alcoholism:
  Alcoholics Anonymous model, 4-6
  behavioral model of, 7-9
  current literature on, 12-13
  medical model of, 6
  Minnesota Model of, 9-11
  models of, 4
  psychoanalytical model of, 7

Alcoholism and Treatment (Armor et al.), 4

Antabuse, 6

Arrests, 128-129

Assessment tools, 87

Attrition, 124-127

Aversion conditioning, 7-8

B

Baumrind, D., 147

Begleiter, H., 6

Behavioral model, 7
  aversion conditioning technique, 7-8
  operant conditioning technique, 8-9

Benson, G., 144

Bias:
  contact, 124
  response, 124-125
  selection, 123-124

Black box design, 35

Blue Cross-Blue Shield of California, 168

Budgeting, follow-up survey, 41-44

C

Cannon, D. S., 8

Capitation contracts, 156

CATOR:
  abstinence after treatment, 121-122
  adolescent outcome, 142-144
  arrests and, 128-129
  attrition and, 124-127
  background, 115-117
  directions for further study, 130-131
  emotional distress and, 129
  job problems and, 128
  medical care utilization rates, 127-128, 171-174
  post-treatment issues, 127-130
  sample description, 117-119
  selection bias and, 123-124
  substance use frequency, 119, 120

treatment stays, 119-121
vocational functioning findings, 175, 176

Chemical Abuse Treatment Registry. See CATOR

Chemical dependency:
cost of not treating, 165-166
defined, 3-4
research on, 19-26

Chi-square, 58

Chronic alcoholism, 4-5

Clerical staff and MIS, 89

Clinical record abstract, 97

Clinical staff and MIS, 89

Coding, 53-55
of pre-treatment data, 55

Computers, 53, 77, 79-80

Confidentiality, 67

Consequences of disease, 24

Consultants, 50, 55
fee-for-service payment method, 63
long-term contract with, 63
mutual expectations, 63-64
software, 88

Contact bias, 124

Control group, 48, 66

Convergent validity, 169-170

Correlation, 58

Cost analyses:
categories of, 155, 157
cost benefit, 163-164
cost containment, 156, 158-160
cost effectiveness, 160-162
cost offset (cost impact), 162-163
in medical care utilization, 167-174
in vocational functioning, 174-177
special issues in, 164-167

Cost benefit analysis, 163-164

Cost containment analysis, 156, 158-160

Cost effectiveness analysis, 160-162

Cost offset analysis, 162-163, 164
cost of not treating chemical dependency, 165-166
in medical care utilization, 167-174
in vocational functioning, 174-177

Cost shifting, 158-159

Cross-tabulation, 57

D

DARP, 137-138

Data:
analyzing, 55-61
gathering during treatment, 45-46
mailed questionnaire, 47
personal interview, 48
presenting and interpreting, 56-60
pre-treatment, 55
reporting, 60-61
telephone interview, 47

Decision making, 78-79

Denial, 21-22

Descriptive statistics, 56

Developmental lag, 147

Diagnosis, 19-20

Difficult populations, 67-68

Documentation, 45-46

Drug Abuse Reporting Program. See DARP

Drug-free outpatient programs, 136

E

Electrical shock, 8

Emerging Concept of Alcohol Dependence, The (Pattison & Sobell), 9

Emetine, 8

Emotional distress, 129

Errors, statistics, 58-59

Escapes, geographical, 22

Ethical issues:

aftercare issues, 67
confidentiality and the right of
    refusal, 67
control group use, 66
notification and the Hawthorne
    Effect, 66-67

Evaluation, 71-72
budgeting for follow-up survey,
    41-44
compared with basic research, 33
defined, 29
follow-up surveys, 34-37
initial planning, 39-41
linking to planning and
    management, 34
outcome evaluation, 32
process evaluation, 31-32
purpose of, 30
types of, 31-32
See also Follow-up evaluation

F

Family of origin, 146, 147

Follow-up evaluation, 34
advantages of, 36-37
attrition and, 124-127
budgeting for, 41-44
coding and computers, 53-55
data analysis, 55-61
data gathering for, 45-46
determining length of, 46-47
initial planning for, 39-41
limitations of, 35-36
methodological concerns about,
    95-97
pre-testing, 61
questionnaire design, 50
questions to ask at, 50-53
reliability measurement, 64-65
research design, 48
response rate, 49-50
sample size, 48-49
sampling problems, 65-66
selection bias and, 123-124
survey methods for, 47-48
validity check, 65

Formative study, 31

Fossheim, I., 144-145

Fuller, Richard K., 95

G

*General Motors-United Auto Workers
    Substance Abuse Program,* 166

Goals, program, 41

H

Harris-Lingoes subscales, 184

Harrison, P. A., 142

Hawthorne Effect, 66-67

Hazelden Evaluation Consortium, 94-95
chemical dependency problem at
    admission, 101-102
client satisfaction with treatment,
    102
elements of, 97-98
methodological concerns, 95-97
patient outcomes, six and twelve
    months after treatment,
    102-111
patient profile, 99-101
program members, 112-113
sample of consortium patients,
    98-99
sample of programs, 98
strength of evaluation, 112
treatment profile, 102, 103

*Hazelden inpatient v. outpatient pro-
    grams,* 181-186

*Hazelden Primary Rehabilitation
    Program,* 94
chemical dependency problem at
    admission, 101-102
client satisfaction with treatment,
    102
elements of evaluation system,
    97-98
methodological concerns, 95-97
patient outcomes, six and twelve
    months after treatment,
    102-111
patient profile, 99-101
treatment profile, 102, 103

*Hazelden study, medical care utiliza-
    tion,* 170-171

Hazelden study, vocational functioning, 174-177

Health care trends, 147-149

Health maintenance organizations (HMOs), 148, 159

Higher Power, 5

Hoffmann, N., 142

Holsten, F., 144-145

Horizontal software, 84

Hospitalization, 127-128

Hubbard, R. L., 138-139

I

Implementation, MIS, 88-90

Inductive statistics, 56

Inferential statistics, 56

Information, 78

Inpatient programs, 162
compared with outpatient programs, 181-186

J

Jellinek, E. M., 4-5

Jellinek Chart, 4-5

Jerrell, 71

Job problems, 128

Joint Commission on the Accreditation of Healthcare Organizations, 32

Juvenile Justice and Delinquency Prevention Act (1974), 148

K

Krueger, Richard A., 95

L

Literature, 12-13

Loss of control, 4

M

MacAndrew Alcoholism Scale, 184

Mailed questionnaire, 47

Management information systems (MIS), 31, 77
assessment tools, 87
consultants used for, 88
defined, 78-79
design of, 82-83
development, three options for, 83-84
evaluation criteria, 84-86
getting started, 81-88
implementation of system, 88-90
information as a resource, 90
prerequisites for development, 80-81
types of systems, 79
what MIS is not, 79-80

Managerial staff and MIS, 89-90

Marlatt, G. A., 9

Martin, J., 147

Medical care utilization, 167-174

Medical model, 6

Microcomputers, 83-84

Minnesota Model, 9-11
treatment outcomes for, 93-113

Minnesota Multiphasic Personality Inventory. See MMPI

MMPI, 181, 183-184

Moselle, K., 147

Moves, healthy, 22

Multzman, I. M., 9

N

Nonopioids, 138

Notification, 66-67

O

Operant conditioning, 8-9

Outcome evaluation, 32
day by day process of, 24-25
linking with quality assurance, 75-76

Outpatient programs, 162
    compared with inpatient programs,
        181-186
    drug-free, 136

Owen, O., 145

P

Packaged software, 84

Patient profile, 99-101

Patient satisfaction-assessment, 97

Pattison, E. M., 9

Patton, 29

Pendery, M. L., 9

*Pennsylvania Substance-Abuse
    System: Uniform Data Collection
    System*. See UDCS

Personal interview, 48

Pittman, 29

Population, 20-21
    difficult, 67-68

Post-treatment follow-up, 97-98

*Preferred provider organizations
    (PPOs)*, 148, 156, 159

Prepaid contracts, 156

Pre-testing, 61

Process evaluation, 31-32

Psychoanalytic model, 7

Publication, right of, 64

Q

Quality assurance, 75-76

Questionnaire, 39
    design of, 50
    mailed, 47

Questions, wording of, 50-53

R

Random sampling, 96

Recovery, 23-24

Regression to the mean, 171-172

Release, right of, 64

Research, compared with evaluation,
    33

Research design, 48

Residential programs, 136

Response bias, 124-125

Response rates, 49-50, 96-97
    AA and NA attendance, six and
        twelve months after treatment,
        108-110
    alcohol and illicit drug use, six and
        twelve months after treatment,
        104-108
    assessment of life quality, six and
        twelve months after treatment,
        110-111
    Hazelden Consortium overall, six
        and twelve months after treat-
        ment, 102-104

Right of refusal, 67

Right of release and publication, 64

S

Sample, 20-21
    Hazelden consortium patients,
        98-99
    Hazelden consortium programs, 98
    random, 96
    setting size of, 48-49

Sampling method, 42, 44
    problems with, 65-66

Schulberg, 71

Selection bias, 123-124

Self-report, 21-22

Sells, S. B., 137

Service bureaus, 83

Shared time, 83

Shock avoidance, 8-9

Significance test, 58

Significant others (S.O.s), 95-96

Simpson, D. D., 137

Slip v. relapse, 22-23

Sobell, L. C., 8-9

Sobell, M. B., 8-9

Social model. See Minnesota Model

Staff, effect of MIS on, 88-90

Statistical Package for Social Sciences (computer program), 53

Statistical regression, 128

Statistics, 56-59

Studies on treatment evaluation 12-13

Success, defining, 69-71

Summative evaluation, 31

T

Technology, 77

Telephone interview, 47

TOPS, 138-140

Treatment cost, 165

Treatment Outcome Prospective Study. See TOPS

U

UDCS, 140-142

Utilization review, 156

V

Vaglum, P., 144-145

Vertical software, 84

Vocational functioning, 174-177

W

Ward, D. A., 11

Wellness programs, 156

West, L. J., 9